ASHE Higher Education Report: Volu... ..., ...
Kelly Ward, Lisa E. Wolf-Wendel, Series Editors

Allies for Inclusion: Disability and Equity in Higher Education

Karen A. Myers

Jaci Jenkins Lindburg

Danielle M. Nied

Allies for Inclusion: Disability and Equity in Higher Education
Karen A. Myers, Jaci Jenkins Lindburg, Danielle M. Nied
ASHE Higher Education Report: Volume 39, Number 5
Kelly Ward, Lisa E. Wolf-Wendel, Series Editors

Cover image by © desuza communications/iStockphoto.
Correction: There was an error in the cover image credit line for 39:4. The cover should have been attributed to © Ela Kwasniewski/iStockphoto.

ISSN 1551-6970 electronic   ISSN 1554-6306   ISBN 978-1-1188-0275-5

The ASHE Higher Education Report is part of the Jossey-Bass Higher and Adult Education Series and is published six times a year by Wiley Subscription Services, Inc., A Wiley Company, at Jossey-Bass, One Montgomery Street, Suite 1200, San Francisco, California 94104-4594.

Individual subscription rate (in USD): $174 per year US/Can/Mex, $210 rest of world; institutional subscription rate: $327 US, $387 Can/Mex, $438 rest of world. Single copy rate: $29. Electronic only–all regions: $174 individual, $327 institutional; Print & Electronic–US: $192 individual, $376 institutional; Print & Electronic–Canada/Mexico: $192 individual, $436 institutional; Print & Electronic–Rest of World: $228 individual, $487 institutional. See the Back Issue/Subscription Order Form in the back of this volume.

CALL FOR PROPOSALS: Prospective authors are strongly encouraged to contact Kelly Ward (kaward@wsu.edu) or Lisa E. Wolf-Wendel (lwolf@ku.edu). See "About the ASHE Higher Education Report Series" in the back of this volume.

Visit the Jossey-Bass Web site at **www.josseybass.com.**

Printed in the United States of America

The ASHE Higher Education Report is indexed in CIJE: Current Index to Journals in Education (ERIC), Education Index/Abstracts (H.W. Wilson), ERIC Database (Education Resources Information Center), Higher Education Abstracts (Claremont Graduate University), IBR & IBZ: International Bibliographies of Periodical Literature (K.G. Saur), and Resources in Education (ERIC).

Advisory Board

The ASHE Higher Education Report Series is sponsored by the Association for the Study of Higher Education (ASHE), which provides an editorial advisory board of ASHE members.

Contents

Executive Summary

This monograph about disability and equity in higher education was designed to provide an overview of students with disabilities in postsecondary institutions and the importance of allies in their lives. With the growth in enrollment of students with diagnosed disabilities, including those who have not disclosed their disabilities to college and university officials, it is imperative for everyone in higher education to know who the students are and how higher education professionals can create welcoming environments for them. Whether students with disabilities are physically on campuses, at satellite campuses, or enrolled in online classes, it is their responsibility to self-advocate. At the same time, it is a *shared* responsibility to provide equitable experiences, which potentially lead to their success. Every member of the higher education community is their ally for inclusion.

Where Disability Is Going

This monograph is a call to action for faculty, staff, and administrators in all facets of higher education. It emphasizes a shared responsibility toward students with disabilities and toward creating meaningful change. The monograph begins with a look into the future of disability education. As Massey (Enterprise Media, 2006) reiterates, we only know where we are going if we know where we have been. Equity, access, inclusion, and awareness are essential components to the success of students and institutions, and they are challenges that must be faced head-on. Shifting the paradigm from viewing disability as a medical condition that needs to be "fixed" to focusing on the lived experience of the individual with a disability through a social, political, and economic lens will move society forward. Through universally designed curriculum, programs, and services, access is provided to all people, erasing the need for specific accommodations and last-minute adjustments. Universal design, universal instructional design, and universal design for student development lead to a future of inclusive practices. Disability studies, an interdisciplinary academic field, allows people to see disability as a social construct rather than a medical deficiency. Globally, countries throughout the world support the United Nations (UN, 2006) Convention on the Rights of Persons with Disabilities, endorsing equal opportunity and a right to education for all people. The UN (2006) Convention, which emphasizes spoken and signed language, inclusive communication, reasonable accommodations, and universal design of products, environments, programs, and services, requires faculty and staff training in these areas, and such professional development is an ongoing endeavor.

Where Disability Has Been

Section 504 of the Rehabilitation Act of 1973 prohibiting discrimination of people with disabilities in federally funded institutions, the Americans with Disabilities Act (ADA) of 1990 prohibiting discrimination of people with disabilities in public and private settings including state and local government, the Americans with Disabilities Act Amendments Act (ADAAA) of 2008 broadening the definition of disability, and the 21st Century Communications and Video Accessibility Act (CCVA) of 2010 ensuring internet accessibility are pieces of disability legislation requiring us to comply with the letter of the law. A multitude of Office of Civil Rights (OCR) complaints and legal cases emerged that called into question discrimination practices, such as *Jenkins v. National Board of Medical Examiners* (2009) regarding a medical student with a learning disability, and Supreme Court cases such as *Southeastern Community College v. Davis* (the first case under Section 504 of the Rehabilitation Act; 1979), regarding a nursing student with a hearing disability, and *University of Alabama v. Garrett* (2001), in which two employees sued the state for discrimination based on their disabilities, resulting in a ruling of state sovereignty in a federal court, are but a few of the cases that set precedence for defining disability and discrimination within higher education. Drawing on theoretical frameworks in multiple disciplines, a central purpose of this monograph is to highlight the status of people with disabilities in United States colleges and universities, and the importance of allies in their lives. Theories such as Gibson's Disability Identity Model; Transition Theory by Schlossberg, Waters, and Goodman; Schlossberg's Theory of Marginality and Mattering; and the Broido Model of Social Justice Ally Development inform practice in higher education.

Where Disability Is Now

In the present day, it is fair to say that disability education and advocacy has come a long way. However, exclusion, albeit often unintentional, is still common for people with disabilities. When and how will higher education get to a place where universal design and proactive accessibility become the norm and accommodation and adjustment become less frequent? The 2013 Daytona 500 was a classic example of where society is today regarding difference in historically believed truths. As Actor James Franco started the race, he knew he could not use the standard phrase "gentlemen, start your engines" since Danica Patrick, a female, was not only a participant but also the lead driver in the race. However, in his last-minute adjustment, he said, "Drivers, and Danica, start your engines." There it was, on a national stage, the very thing that people with disabilities live on a daily basis—an afterthought to inclusion.

Through messages like this monograph, and through increasing outreach and exposure to disability through venues like *Allies for Inclusion: The Ability Exhibit*, people may better understand disability, and at the same time, understand why disability truly is a social construct. In addition, these messages should be delivered through the continued development of allies—the people who "see themselves as equal to those with and without disabilities [and who are] committed to eliminating negative attitudes, stereotypes, and oppressive behaviors" (Casey-Powell & Souma, 2009, p. 162).

Foreword

College students bring with them to educational experiences a composite of who they are in terms of physical wellness, mental well-being, emotional readiness, cultural and family background, as well as different aspects of identity. Students with disabilities are an important part of the higher educational landscape and meeting their needs is vital to the growth and development of students with disability as well as the campuses where they work and study. In their monograph *Allies for Inclusion: Disability and Equity in Higher Education*, Karen A. Myers, Jaci Jenkins Lindburg, and Danielle M. Nied do a laudable job of providing much needed foundational information related to all aspects of disability education. The authors embed the topic of students with disability in the larger milieu of student development and diversity including discussions of power, privilege, and difference.

As with many aspects of student identity, students with disabilities are often overlooked and/or misunderstood because people do not recognize the nuances of identity and how it can impact the college-going experience. Even well-meaning people can be fearful of saying or doing the wrong thing when it comes to working with students with different types of disabilities. Political correctness can paralyze effective action and practice when it comes to creating inclusive campus environments. Further, topics related to disability can easily be overlooked or marginalized with people thinking disability issues and concerns are addressed by the office on campus that deals with students with disabilities. The challenge with such an outlook is that students with disabilities, many of them invisible, are part of all aspects of campus. All members of the campus need to know about issues associated with disabilities. The authors encourage an approach to inclusion that is grounded in shared responsibility. Disability education is not just for staff members who work in disabilities service offices or professors of disability studies. Disability education is the responsibility of all members of the campus community. As the authors advocate, "everyone is an ally for inclusion."

The *Allies for Inclusion* monograph provides a great resource to help create campus environments that are welcoming, open, affirming, and inclusive of students with different forms of disability. The information contained in the monograph is accessible and easy to read. Readers will find topics ranging from legal issues to working with students with different types of disabilities as well as topics associated with curriculum, classrooms, and campus environments. The book is particularly timely given concerns about mental health and creating campus environments that are healthy, open, and diverse. The book is useful and practical in its specificity about how to handle different situations involving students with disabilities and addressing the needs of students with different types of disabilities. Using the literature, the authors frame issues associated with disability in larger discourses related to diversity and access.

All members of the campus community can benefit from reading this monograph. Faculty and staff who work with students will find the background and practical information related to working with students with a range of disabilities useful, practical, and critical to effective practice. Staff in offices that work to support students with disabilities will also benefit from reading the monograph. Every office of disability services should have a copy of the monograph on their bookshelf to support their work with students and the faculty and staff that work with students. The monograph is also a great professional development tool to help faculty, staff, and students realize the gamut of disabilities and to understand foundational issues and effective practice. The monograph is also sure to be of use to faculty and students associated with disabilities research as well as those who study student access and diversity. Classes inclusive of topics related to legal issues in higher education, student development, access, and disabilities studies will also find the monograph an important component of a comprehensive reading list.

Throughout the past five years, the ASHE Monograph Series has been intentional to include topics related to different aspects of student development, diversity, and access, The *Allies for Inclusion* monograph stands beside other monographs in the series like *Piecing Together the Student Success Puzzle: Research, Propositions, and Recommendations* by Kuh, Kinzie, Buckley, Bridges, and Hayek as well as *Postsecondary Education for American Indian and Alaska Natives: Higher Education for Nation Building and Self-Determination* by Brayboy, Fann, Castagno, and Solyom in addition *to Latinos in Higher Education: Creating Conditions for Student Success* by Nuñez, Hoover, Pickett, Stuart-Carruthers, and Vazquez and *Stonewall's Legacy: Bisexual, Gay, Lesbian, and Transgender Students in Higher Education* by Marine. The intent of such a compendium of resources is to contribute information to the improvement of campus practice and policy that promotes inclusion and this is clear that all members of the campus community play a role in fostering student success for all students.

Students with disabilities are not a monolith. Disability has a broad scope and encompasses physical, mental, and psychological conditions that are both visible and invisible. The authors address the range of experience encompassed by the term disability and associated reasonable accommodation. The information the authors provide in the *Allies for Inclusion* monograph is informative, well-grounded, and practical, and sure to be of use to readers.

Acknowledgments

We wish to express our heartfelt thanks to Claire Minneman, our outstanding graduate student, who gave an extraordinary amount of her time to assist us with editing this monograph in its early stages. We are grateful to Kelly Willerding, Sister Thu Do, and Alisha Abbott who provided research assistance, to Sarah Laux who provided copy editing, and to our families and friends who provided ongoing encouragement, patience, and support. Our sincere thanks go to all the people with disabilities and their allies who continue the march for inclusion.

Published online in Wiley Online Library
(wileyonlinelibrary.com) • DOI: 10.1002/aehe.20011

The Future of Equity and Inclusion: Creating Meaningful Change

> What you are is where you were when
> Dr. Morris Massey (Enterprise Media, 1972)

WHERE WERE YOU WHEN YOU FIRST experienced disability? Was it real life? Do you remember your great-grandfather's hands shaking as he tried to feed himself? Did you notice a young woman on the bus wearing dark glasses and using a white cane? Did you see people get out of their wheelchairs and crawl up the steps of the Capitol building on the national news? Or, was it fiction? Did you watch Mary on *Little House on the Prairie*, Kevin in *Joan of Arcadia*, *Pollyanna*, *Forrest Gump*, or *The Elephant Man*? Did the actors themselves have disabilities such as Gerri in *Facts of Life*, Corky in *Life Goes On*, or Marlee Matlin in *Children of a Lesser God*? If what sociologist Morris Massey said is true, if "What you are is where you were when" (which is the title of his 1972 video), then our perceptions of disability developed at the moment we first remember experiencing, witnessing, or seeing disability. Are these perceptions the same as they were then, or have they developed, grown, or changed over time?

This monograph begins with a discussion of the future of equity and inclusion. If disability is to ever be perceived differently, then meaningful change must be created. In order to determine what the meaningful change will be, it must first be examined why change should occur, then what that change should be and how to make that change happen.

It has been over 20 years since the signing of the Americans with Disabilities Act (ADA) of 1990 (Public Law 101–336, 1990) and 40 years since the Rehabilitation Act of 1973 (Public Law 93–112, 1973). Both of these laws protect against discrimination of people with disabilities by requiring equal access to employment, education, goods, and services. In 2010, nearly one in five Americans, 56.7 million people, reported having a disability (Brault, 2012, p. 4), and that number is growing. The percentage of high-school graduates with disabilities matriculating to college has increased from 3% in 1978 to 19% in 1996, and the number of students with disabilities attending colleges and universities has more than tripled over the last 30 years from 3% in 1978 to 9% in 1998 and 11% in 2008 (Snyder & Dillow, 2010; United States Department of Education, National Center for Education Statistics [ED NCES], 2006). Yet, as reported by the National Center for Education Statistics (ED NCES, 2006), nearly half (47%) of students with disabilities leave college without completing a degree compared to approximately 36% of their counterparts without disabilities failing to graduate. (*Authors' note*: these statistics are not recent; it is important to indicate at the outset that disability statistics vary from source to source and are not readily available, thus supporting the call for future research in the area of disability in higher education.)

Over the years, Americans have progressed in their attitudes and behaviors toward people with disabilities. As addressed throughout this monograph, disability education on the college level has evolved from classes and degrees in special education and rehabilitation with strong emphases on the medical model of disability in the 1960s to the incorporation of the topic of disability in diversity classes modeling a minority group model of disability in the 1990s (Jones, 1996). In the 21st century, interdisciplinary degrees in disability studies emerged focusing on the social construction of disability, intending to epistemologically and practically move away from onus on the person with the disability to onus on society and the barriers in which it constructs (Linton, 1998, 2007). Federal legislation such as the Civil Rights Act of 1964, Section 504 of the Rehabilitation Act of 1973, and the Americans with Disabilities Act (ADA) of 1990 has made higher education more available to historically underrepresented groups of many types. However, educational practices and culture have not extensively shifted to address the experiences and learning needs of newly enrolled students. In their article "Historical, Theoretical, and Foundational Principles of Universal Instructional Design in Higher Education," Pliner and Johnson (2004) state that the absence of efforts to change the culture of practices in higher education has "created significant barriers to access, retention, and graduation for many students," particularly those with disabilities, thus creating higher attrition rates among this student population (p. 106).

Despite the growth and development of disability education, antiquated thoughts and practices still exist within society. For example, signs indicating "Handicapped Parking" still litter parking lots; labels indicating "Handicapped Entrance" are posted at ramped areas of public buildings; and public restrooms labeling stalls with handrails as "Handicap-Accessible" are still prevalent. Such signage not only uses outdated language but it also emphasizes and reinforces the "us" and "them" mentality—the "us"—people without disabilities who may use the "normal" facilities and services—and the "them"—people with disabilities who are "different" and "in need" of assistance.

Language is instrumental in demonstrating the attitudes and beliefs of human beings. How a society perceives its members is established through its language. Using outdated and seemingly offensive labels such as "handicapped" indicates the view of a particular culture toward its members with disabilities (Linton, 1998; Tregoning, 2009). Such perceptions are then carried out through behaviors. Instead of emphasizing differences and deficits through negative labels, focusing on the person and using person-first language, that is, a woman with a disability rather than "a handicapped or disabled woman," provides respect and dignity. As a society, America can be proud of its advances in medicine, science, technology, and education. Through these advances, Americans have changed the perception of disability from one of deficit and need to one of strength and power. Aimee Mullins is an athlete and model who, with no legs, has won marathons and broken records at the Paralympic Games. In her TED talk, Mullins (2009) addressed the audience, saying "The conversation with society has changed profoundly over the past decade … from a conversation of deficiency to one about augmentation and potential."

Through highly technical prosthetics that augment human limbs for walking, running, grasping, and throwing, and electronic devices used for seeing, hearing, and speaking, people with disabilities have chosen to change the way society views them.

So what is the status today in higher education? How has society grown in understanding disability, what are the key issues that remain today, and where is disability headed in the future at colleges and universities in the United States? Although disability education has evolved and awareness is much greater than it was 10 or 20 years ago, there are still questions and there remains work to be done. Individuals with disabilities continue to be a mystery to people without disabilities. Most college professionals recognize that disability legislation exists and must be followed, though it is common for faculty, staff, and administrators to assume that "those people" are the responsibility of disability services, human resources, and affirmative action offices. Cases such as *Jenkins v. National Board of Medical Examiners* (2009) indicate that higher education institutions continue to discriminate against students with disabilities, seeing them as deficient or unable to meet standards. This may come from lack of awareness, negative attitudes of people toward individuals with disabilities, lack of allies, antiquated policies, and practices, and so forth. As a result, students—particularly those with invisible or "hidden" disabilities—tend not to disclose their disabilities, fearing embarrassment, retribution, marginality, and failure (Olney & Brockelman, 2003; Tripoli, Mellard, & Kurth, 2004).

Although research and scholarship related to people with disabilities continues to grow, it remains limited. Attitudes toward students with disabilities and their accommodations, for example, indicate less concern toward people with physical disabilities than with learning and psychological disabilities (Meyer, Myers, Walmsley, & Laux, 2012; Myers, Jenkins, & Pousson, 2009; Upton, Harper, & Wadsworth, 2005). Questions regarding the legitimacy of disability and the need for accommodations arise from faculty and employers. Student satisfaction of disability services shows overall satisfaction with disability services staff; however, students with disabilities express concern about faculty understanding and utilizing inclusive teaching practices (Myers & Bastian, 2010).

With the increasing number of college students with disabilities, that is, approximately 11% of college students (Raue & Lewis, 2011; ED NCES, 2006) and the increasing number of individuals with disabilities in our communities, that is, 18.7% (Brault, 2012, p. 4), awareness of disability issues and how to communicate comfortably with people with disabilities is essential for practitioners and educators. Uncomfortable interactions and misinformation between members of the campus community with and without disabilities result in people with disabilities becoming marginalized. Lack of equity can have broad-reaching consequences for quality of life, learning environments in and outside the classroom, and career experiences for college students and employees with disabilities.

Equity for people with disabilities has yet to be achieved despite decades of activism and legislation. Although the number of college students and staff who disclose disabilities is growing in the United States, the attitudes and perceptions toward people with disabilities have not advanced at a similar pace. Stigmas and stereotypes of people with disabilities as "less than" and "not equal to" continue to be shown by faculty, administrators, staff, and students. The comfort level between individuals with and without disabilities remains out of balance, and questions and concerns continue about appropriate communication, comfort level, and inclusive practices. When it comes to interacting with individuals with disabilities, members of the campus community still have questions regarding appropriate communication, expected behavior, and their roles in the process. This monograph attempts to answer some of these questions.

An enhanced understanding of the social forces shaping understandings of disability equity provides readers with a new lens through which to examine the status of people with disabilities in higher education. Utilizing models and theoretical frameworks of marginality and mattering (Schlossberg, 1989), disability identity development (Gibson, 2006, 2011), and universal instructional design (Higbee, 2003; Higbee & Goff, 2008), this monograph addresses people with disabilities on college campuses—students, faculty, and staff—thus providing a more holistic and realistic picture. Exploring current issues of inequity and inclusion, this publication will serve as a guide to promote the inclusion of people with disabilities.

Disability Defined: What Does It Mean?

It is important to have an understanding and create a shared meaning of several fundamental concepts when considering disability and equity in higher education. The term "disability" itself may have multiple meanings depending on the source and audience. In the Americans with Disabilities Act (1990), disability is defined as "a physical or mental impairment that substantially limits one or more of the major life activities . . . ; a record of such an impairment; or being regarded as having such an impairment regardless of whether the individual actually has the impairment." According to Oliver (1996) and Disabled Peoples International (as cited in Oliver), disability is defined as "the loss or limitation of opportunities to take part in the normal life of the community on an equal level with others due to physical and social barriers" (p. 41). Impairment, on the other hand, is the "functional limitation within the individual caused by physical, mental, or sensory impairment" (p. 41). Based on Oliver's definitions, disability is a systemic phenomenon and does not refer to a person's body (Gilson, 2000). Similar to Gilson's definition, and for the purpose of the current discussion in this monograph, disability is viewed as a social construct, taking into account the full lived experience in terms of the functional limitations and the social, cultural, and political consequences. Disability may be affected by multiple factors and may include multiple identities. The key terms defined in this chapter include access, equity, climate, discrimination, inclusion, accommodations, modifications, affirmative action, and auxiliary aids.

Within the context of this monograph, the term *access* refers to the process of entering a postsecondary institution or an individual's ability to come into the higher education arena. It is important to consider common barriers to accessing higher education, which include but are not limited to high cost, work requirements, family/home demands, academic ability, individual merit, a lacking support system, and inadequate information about policies, aid, and college life in general.

The term *equity* refers to fairness, impartiality, and justness. When considering equity within the context of higher education, it includes references of social justice and an equal opportunity for all people to enter higher education, regardless of their socioeconomic status, ability or disability, race, gender, culture, or background.

Discrimination refers to the unfair or prejudicial treatment of an individual based on perceived or actual characteristics. It is the act of unjustly or unfairly making a distinction or consideration about a person based on the larger group, class, or category to which they belong rather than evaluating an individual on their own personal traits, qualities, and merits. Within the scope of higher education, discrimination can take many forms, including, but not limited to, discrimination based on one's race, socioeconomic status, gender, age, culture, religion, disability, or even peer group.

The term *inclusion* refers to all-encompassing access to admission, programs, events, classes, and physical spaces within the college and university environment. An inclusive program on campus would be one that could easily be attended by anyone, regardless of his or her physical, mental, or psychological characteristics. An example of an inclusive practice used in the higher education sector is universal design (UD). As defined by Ron Mace, founder and program director of The Center for Universal Design, UD is "the design of products and environments to be usable by all people, to the greatest extent possible, without the need for adaptation or specialized design" (North Carolina State University, 2008, para. 1). For example, an instructor would be embracing UD if they used large-print font on all course handouts, ensuring that all students in the class could read the content, regardless of whether or not the student had a visual disability. To be inclusive, one must be proactive and thoughtful to the needs of all persons. Inclusion happens ahead of time, rather than being reactionary.

In contrast, an *accommodation* or *modification* is an adjustment made to a course, program, event, service, job, activity, or physical space that enables individuals with disabilities to participate equally. These accommodations or modifications occur after an individual with a disability has discovered that the current environment is prohibitive of their full participation. A college or university deems an accommodation "reasonable" when it is appropriate, effective, and efficient, and is agreed upon by the appropriate representative of the institution, as well as the individual with a disability. Common types of accommodation available for students with disabilities in the postsecondary environment include, but are not limited to, additional time to complete exams or written work, captioning services, alternative exam formats, note-taking services, sign language interpreters, tape recorders, and modified graduation requirements (University of Massachusetts Amherst, 2011). An *auxiliary aid* is an accommodation for students with sensory, manual, or speaking disabilities that seeks to equalize the opportunity to participate in classes, programs, or activities (Office for Civil Rights, 1998a). An example of an auxiliary aid is an audio textbook, screen reader, talking calculator, or voice synthesizer. Section 504 of the Rehabilitation Act and the Americans with Disabilities Act include stipulations for the provision of auxiliary aids and services.

The final term that is important to define within this monograph is affirmative action. *Affirmative action* is a policy that considers an individual's race, culture, religion, gender, sexual orientation, disability, or veteran status, and seeks to benefit an underrepresented group within educational entities, businesses, and other forms of employment. Affirmative action dates back to the early 1960s, when the government began to promote actions that achieved nondiscrimination. Affirmative action policies are designed to provide opportunities for defined groups. Within the college and university environment, affirmative action is commonly discussed in processes such as the selection of students for admission, the awarding of scholarship and grant opportunities, and the recruitment and hiring of employees.

Overview of the Monograph

Equity, access, inclusion, and awareness are ongoing challenges related to disability in higher education. It is imperative to initiate a call to action for faculty, staff, and administrators in all facets of higher education to see disability as something for which everyone is responsible. Creating meaningful change in the future is based on how disability has been conceived in the past, how disability is understood today, and where disability in higher education is headed in the future. Drawing upon theoretical frameworks informed by interdisciplinary scholarship—including psychology, sociology, education, disability studies, and rehabilitation—a central purpose of this monograph is to highlight the status of people with disabilities in United States colleges and universities, and the importance of allies in their lives. According to Casey-Powell and Souma (2009) in Higbee and Mitchell's *Making Good on the Promise: Student Affairs Professionals with Disabilities*, allies are people who "see themselves as equal to those with and without disabilities . . . committed to eliminating negative attitudes, stereotypes, and oppressive behaviors" (p. 162).

The intent of this monograph is to summarize policy and some of the literature and research on disability. However, certain aspects of the literature are very limited, as research does not yet exist on some of the specific topics at present time. Throughout this monograph, recommended suggestions for future research are provided.

The status of individuals with disabilities in higher education is examined from several perspectives including historical progress, legislation, litigation, attitudes, perceptions, statistics, types of disabilities, and service provisions. In addition, the purpose, roles, and necessary actions of allies are emphasized and innovations shaping the new disability movement are explored.

Allies for Inclusion: Disability and Equity in Higher Education highlights the status of people with disabilities in United States colleges and universities and the importance of allies in their lives. By attempting to deflate common myths that contribute to the exclusion of people with disabilities and offering strategies for continued progress toward equity and inclusion, this monograph serves as a guide to promote the inclusion of people with disabilities.

The next chapter, *A Historical Overview of the Disability Movement*, provides an overview of the history of disability in higher education and society. This chapter discusses key pieces of legislation, cases, decisions, and policies in the law that helped shape the disability movement.

The third chapter, *Disabilities of College Campuses: An Overview*, provides a general synopsis of the status of disability in United States higher education and arenas for examining disability access. Types of disabilities, differences within types of disabilities, types of accommodations, and who are receiving accommodations are addressed.

The fourth chapter, *Understanding Campus Complexity: Problems, Challenges, and Marginalization*, provides an examination of the problems and challenges faced by people with disabilities in higher education. A review of the literature and relevant scholarly perspectives and theories regarding disability and equity within higher education are discussed, together with activities and actions leading to marginalization and its impact on students, faculty, administration, and staff. This chapter also addresses the shift from the medical model of disability to the social model of disability and deflates the myths regarding disability in higher education.

The fifth chapter, *Increasing Awareness: Allies, Advocacy, and the Campus Community*, provides information and perspectives for allies of people with disabilities. It attempts to answer the question "How can others advocate for people with disabilities?" in our everyday lives on college campuses. More specifically, the chapter conceptualizes the importance of allies of people with disabilities, advocacy, and activism on college campuses. It poses key questions for both in-group and out-of-group allies, emphasizing the importance of each, provides an analysis of advocacy for disability in society and on college campuses, and offers an in-depth look at the ways in which their campus communities affect individuals with disabilities. The concept of praxis, that is, taking allies from knowledge acquisition to action, is explored.

The sixth chapter, *Increasing Awareness: Language, Communication Strategies, and Universally Designed Environments*, examines ways to increase awareness of people with disabilities using language and communication strategies. Research that provides insight into best practices for communicating with people with disabilities is explored. This chapter also introduces and discusses universal instructional design and promotes its implementation both in and outside the classroom on college campuses.

The final chapter, *The New Movement in Disability Education and Advocacy*, provides a look at the current state of disability education and advocacy within higher education as well as analyzes several new programs and initiatives being implemented on specific campuses. The chapter discusses new movements in disability such as *Allies for Inclusion: The Ability Exhibit* (Saint Louis University) and PASS-IT (University of Minnesota), and the continued outreach of DO-IT (University of Washington), Aimee Mullins, Temple Grandin, and others. Current strategies to eliminate inequity for people with disabilities are addressed; gaps and ongoing challenges are identified; and in light of theoretical frameworks, promising efforts to fill the gaps and tackle ongoing challenges are offered.

Disability education is *for* everyone *by* everyone. It is a shared responsibility, and it is up to each person to model inclusive behavior (Bryan & Myers, 2006). In exploring the past, present, and future of disability in higher education and experiencing its transformation in these pages, the theme of "shared responsibility" is threaded throughout. Disability education is not for the chosen few who are service providers and professors of disability studies; rather, disability education is the responsibility of each member of the campus community. Everyone is an ally for inclusion.

A Historical Overview of the Disability Movement

> We must be the advocates of hope and challenge when barriers are imposed on individuals with disabilities restricting their access to a full and inclusive life.
>
> Dan Snobl (Yost, 2008, para. 29)

THE DISABILITY MOVEMENT IN THE United States has its roots in the mid-1800s and continues to evolve in present day. Through citizen activism, political efforts, and widespread awareness campaigns, the disability movement swept the nation in a similar fashion to the Civil Rights and Women's Rights Movements. Marked with periods of profound stereotyping and apparent discrimination, people with disabilities now have defined rights and responsibilities under fundamental pieces of legislation and key court cases decided in the last half century. This chapter takes a closer look at the important definitions, policies, and laws that form the basis of the disability movement, and summarizes the decisions of seven key court cases that have established precedence for colleges and universities when working with people with disabilities.

Key Definitions and Early Policies

In order to gain a better understanding of disability in higher education and society today, it is critical to first look at the key policies and laws that shaped the disability movement and rights for people with disabilities in the United States. Additionally, it is crucial to grasp what disability truly is, both in a legal and social construct.

Definitions

It is common for people to have an inaccurate picture of disabilities. Frequently, a person will define disability in terms of their own familiarity or exposure; for example, if a coworker uses a wheelchair, someone might believe disabilities are only physical in nature. In reality, disabilities can be physical, mental, or psychological. Disabilities can also be visible, such as multiple sclerosis, or invisible, such as dyslexia. As stated in the previous chapter, the legal definition of "disability" has been outlined in Section 504 of the Rehabilitation Act of 1973 and the Americans with Disabilities Act, both of which are discussed in greater detail later in this chapter. According to Section 504, individuals with disabilities are defined as "persons with a physical or mental impairment which substantially limits one or more major life activities. Major life activities include caring for one's self, walking, seeing, hearing, speaking, breathing, working, performing manual tasks, and learning" (United States Department of Health and Human Services, 2006, para. 3).

Disability also has been defined under the Americans with Disabilities Act (ADA), signed into law in 1990. According to this Act, an individual is considered to have a disability if "s/he has a physical or mental impairment that substantially limits one or more major life activities, has a record of such an impairment, or is regarded as having such an impairment" (United States Department of Justice, 2002, para. 6). Characterizing "disability" differs substantially from defining "disabled" or "impairment." Terms such as "disabled" or "impairment" focus on the condition itself and are generally more offensive than using person-first language (i.e., he is a "student with a disability"), which emphasizes the individual and not the condition. Terms such as "handicapped" also place focus on the condition whereas using the term "accessible" emphasizes a positive, intentional accommodation that works for all people, regardless of the presence of a disability.

Early Policies and the Spirit of Change

The conversation about disability in society and, specifically, in higher education, dates back to the 1860s, when Abraham Lincoln established the legislation that funded Washington DC's Gallaudet University, a school for deaf students. As Jane Jarrow (1993) describes, "More than 130 years ago, people in the United States recognized that an individual with a disability was not incapable of thinking, learning, or achieving" (p. 5). It would be nearly 100 years before the movement gained major momentum with the passing of the Civil Rights Act of 1964, Title IX in 1972, and the Rehabilitation Act of 1973.

The country was stirring with the spirit of change in the late 1950s and early 1960s. Social movements, major campaigns of civil resistance, acts of nonviolent protest, civil disobedience, boycotts, sit-ins, and eventually racially motivated violence sprang up in response to civil rights issues of inequality. Many Americans were calling for change and outwardly expressing a desire for equality in terms of race and gender. This movement gained major momentum with the election of Democratic President John F. Kennedy in 1961. The President worked diligently to pass "imperative" legislation that would give all Americans the right to be served in public facilities including hotels, restaurants, theaters, and retail stores, as well as protect voting privileges. Upon assuming office in late 1963, President Lyndon Johnson wanted to pass the Civil Rights Act as swiftly as possible and it was ultimately signed into law on July 2, 1964. This piece of legislation was and continues to be the nation's benchmark regarding civil rights, as it prohibits discrimination on the basis of race, color, religion, sex, or national origin (United States Senate Committee on the Judiciary, 2013). Although this legislation did not directly address equal rights of people with disabilities, it certainly paved the way for future anti-discrimination legislation, including rights for women in Title IX and rights for people with disabilities in the Rehabilitation Act.

Several years after the Civil Rights Act was passed, Title IX began to take shape when Bernice Sandler began to fight for a faculty position at the University of Maryland in 1969. Sandler was able to demonstrate inequalities in pay, rank, and hiring between women and men in the higher education sector. Eventually, she filed the famous class action complaint against all universities and colleges in the country with explicit charges naming the University of Maryland (B. R. Sandler, 1997). When Title IX passed in 1972, it required gender equity within every educational program receiving funding from the federal government. Specifically, it states, "No person in the United States shall, on the basis of sex, be excluded from participation in, be denied the benefits of, or be subjected to discrimination under any education program or activity receiving federal financial assistance" (Office for Civil Rights, 1998b, para. 1). Title IX addresses 10 key areas, including athletics, access to higher education, career education, education for pregnant/parenting students, employment, learning environment, math and science, sexual harassment, and standardized testing and technology (Titleix.info, 2013). In a similar way to the Civil Rights Act of 1964, Title IX did not directly impact people with disabilities, but the energy surrounding equal rights in the United States continued to build as a result of its passage.

Groundbreaking Legislation: The Rehabilitation Act and ADA

Disability legislation intended to protect the rights of people with disabilities in the United States has been in place for over 40 years. Explanations of two of these laws that specifically protect college students are provided below.

Section 504 of the Rehabilitation Act of 1973

Nine years after the Civil Rights Act and just one year after Title IX was passed, the Rehabilitation Act of 1973 was passed by Congress. One subsection of this act, Section 504, is widely regarded as the first national civil rights legislation for Americans with disabilities (Jarrow, 1993). In short, the legislation is a national law that protects qualified individuals from being discriminated against due to their disability (United States Department of Health and Human Services, 2006). The law states that "no otherwise qualified individual with a disability in the United States shall, solely by reason of disability, be excluded from participation in, be denied the benefits of, or be subjected to discrimination under any program or activity receiving federal financial assistance" (29 U.S.C. 794). Concerns about cost caused a delay in the policy's application for several years and it wasn't until a series of highly visible protests in 1977 that government officials finally issued regulations and implementation guidelines for the Rehabilitation Act to go into practice across the nation. As Jane Jarrow (1993) eloquently states, "For people with disabilities in the United States, Section 504 means more than access to opportunity. It holds out the promise of dignity in pursuit of basic rights of safety and independence. Prior to Section 504, the provision of services and support for people with disabilities was largely the result of whim—pity, guilt, or obligation. Section 504 recognized that the functional limitations engendered by disability did not diminish the individual's status as a person whose right to life, liberty, and the pursuit of happiness is guaranteed by law" (p. 8).

As Section 504 took effect, federally funded institutions including public colleges and universities were now required to comply with its standards for equal treatment of people with disabilities. In addition, private colleges and universities were required to act in accordance with Section 504 since their students receive federal funds. Section 504 contains a series of specific regulatory provisions regarding student services on a college campus (Heyward, 1993). Through a series of lawsuits discussed later in this chapter, it was determined that schools were not complying with these mandates, which ultimately led to the passage of the Americans with Disabilities Act of 1990.

Americans With Disabilities Act of 1990

Considered to be the most "sweeping piece of civil rights legislation passed in more than twenty-five years" (Jarrow, 1993, p. 15), the Americans with Disabilities Act (ADA) was signed into law by President H. W. Bush in July 1990. The law was very much a joint effort of both political parties, all branches of federal and state government, and Americans with and without disabilities. When the President signed the Act into law, he stated: "Let the shameful walls of exclusion finally come tumbling down," summarizing the key message of the Act: "that millions of Americans with disabilities are full-fledged

TABLE 1
Americans With Disabilities Act of 1990

Title of the ADA	Coverage
Title I	Equal employment opportunities
Title II	Nondiscrimination in public programs, services, and activities
Title III	Accommodation in all public and privately owned services
Title IV	Telephone companies must provide telecommunication relay services
Title V	Miscellaneous provisions, including state immunity, retaliation, attorney's fees, coverage of Congress, relationship to other laws, and the impact on insurance providers

citizens and, as such, are entitled to legal protections that ensure them equal opportunity and access to the mainstream of American life" (Texas A&M, 2013, para. 5). This law extended the scope of nondiscrimination for persons with disabilities to a wider array of areas, including the private sector, employment, public services, public accommodations, telecommunications, transportation, and other miscellaneous provisions (White House Press Secretary, 1990). As a result, all entities in the United States besides churches and private country clubs are now required to adhere to the ADA.

There are five titles of the Americans with Disabilities Act. Table 1 outlines these five titles.

Title I addresses the equal employment opportunity for individuals with disabilities. This title is designed to "remove barriers that would deny qualified individuals with disabilities access to the same employment opportunities and benefits available to others without disabilities. Employers must reasonably accommodate the disabilities of qualified applicants or employees, unless an undue hardship would result" (Disability Access Consultants [DAC], 2012, para. 1). Under Title I, a person with a disability must be given the same consideration for employment that is given to a person without a disability, so long as the person with a disability is qualified for the employment opportunity (Kentucky's Office for the Americans with Disabilities Act [KYADA], 2007). Title I must be adhered to by all entities in the United States, with the exception of employers with less than

15 employees, the executive branch of the Federal Government, private clubs, churches, and Native American reservations.

Title II of the Americans with Disabilities Act addresses right to access of public services by people with disabilities. Under this portion of the Act, people with disabilities should have access to "all services, programs, and activities provided or made available by local or state governments and their affiliate agencies . . . regardless of A) whether they receive federal funding, and B) how many employees they have" (KYADA, 2007, para. 3). Some examples of public services that are covered by Title II of the ADA include state parks, schools and universities, public transportation, and the government proceedings. One of the most noteworthy aspects of Title II is the protection offered to people with disabilities who wish to participate in higher education. The ADA protects individuals from being denied the opportunity to participate; however, the law does not require institutions to accept or accommodate everyone with a disability (KYADA, 2007).

The ADA (and Section 504 of the Rehabilitation Act) established both rights and responsibilities of persons with disabilities participating in higher education. As Heyward (1993) discusses, a person with a disability has the right to nondiscrimination and meaningful access, yet also has the responsibility to request reasonable modifications be made on their behalf. An individual has the right to personalized assessments, but also has a responsibility to meet eligibility standards detailing the qualified status. A person with a disability has the right to effective academic adjustments and aids, but also has a responsibility to provide documentation to representatives at the institution. And finally, a person with a disability has the right to confidentiality, yet also has the responsibility to provide necessary information when requested. A great deal of these rights and responsibilities of people with disabilities in higher education were established through a series of court cases, which is discussed later in this chapter.

Title III of the Americans with Disabilities Act prohibits the discrimination of people with disabilities by private entities in places of public accommodation. Before the passage of the ADA, accommodations were only required for entities receiving federal funds. Title III expanded upon that and now requires all new places of public accommodation, including commercial facilities, "to be designed and constructed so as to be readily accessible and usable by persons with disabilities" (KYADA, 2007, para. 4). Examples of private entities referred to by the Act include restaurants, bars, movie theatres, hotels, and retail stores. It is important to note that Title III refers to "new" facilities and not existing facilities. Existing facilities are expected to remove physical barriers when it can be accomplished easily and without a great expense to the owner. In addition, Title III does not require entities to alter the nature of their services in order to meet the accommodation. As KYADA (2007) describes, "a dimly lit romantic restaurant would not be required to increase their lighting as an accommodation, since doing so would destroy the intended ambience of the business" (para. 5).

Title IV of the ADA addresses telecommunications. This title requires telephone companies to have "interstate and intrastate telephone relay services in every state" (DAC, 2012, para. 4). The relay services must provide "speech-impaired or hearing impaired individuals who use TDDs (Telecommunication Device for the Deaf) or other non-voice terminal devices opportunities for communication that are equivalent to those provided to other customers" (KYADA, 2007, para. 6).

And finally, Title V of the ADA includes a wide range of miscellaneous provisions. As one might imagine, retaliation becomes very important for people with disabilities when it comes to legal rights for accommodation and nondiscrimination. Title V protects people with disabilities from being retaliated against after successfully suing an entity. The person with a disability, as well as anyone who may have testified on the disabled individual's behalf, is also protected from threats and harassment. Title V outlines an individual's ability to sue a state, as well as the federal government, for failure to comply with the ADA. Under Title V, an individual can bring charges against a state, but no damages will be awarded; whereas the federal government can sue any state, with financial penalties attached.

The ADA uses several phrases extensively, including person with a disability, qualified individual, reasonable accommodation, and major life activities. As was discussed earlier in this chapter, according to the ADA, an individual is considered to have a disability if "s/he has a physical or mental impairment that substantially limits one or more major life activities, has a record of such an impairment, or is regarded as having such an impairment" (United States Department of Justice, 2002, para. 6). A major life activity is a substantial virtue, such as seeing, hearing, speaking, walking, breathing, performing manual tasks, learning, caring for oneself, and working (United States Equal Employment Opportunity Commission [EEOC], 1997). A "qualified individual" is "an individual with a disability who, with or without reasonable accommodation, can perform the essential functions of the employment position that such individual holds or desires" (Kaplin & Lee, 2007, p. 151). A reasonable accommodation is "any change or adjustment to a job or work environment that permits a qualified applicant or employee with a disability to participate in the job application process, to perform the essential functions of a job, or to enjoy benefits and privileges of employment equal to those enjoyed by employees without disabilities" (Business and Legal Resources [BLR], 2013, para. 7).

It is important to note that the ADA expanded upon Section 504 of the Rehabilitation Act, but it did not take the place of it. Thus, postsecondary institutions (and other entities) are held to the mandates in both pieces of legislation. For higher education, the main result of the passage of the ADA was an increased institutional and public awareness of disability-related issues.

Discussion of Key Court Cases

Under Section 504 of the Rehabilitation Act and the Americans with Disabilities Act (ADA), rights and responsibilities of people with disabilities were determined and discrimination against people with disabilities was prohibited. However, as these pieces of legislation were enacted by the executive and legislative branches of government, the judicial branch was also experiencing legal actions brought forth against colleges and universities by people with disabilities. "Courts interpreting Section 504 have clarified some of the questions regarding the procedural and substantive issues that its legislative history and regulations left unanswered" (Hurley, 1991, p. 1062). These landmark cases helped determine a precedent for people with disabilities in higher education.

Southeastern Community College v. Davis (1979)

The first case, *Southeastern Community College v. Davis* (1979), saw the United States Supreme Court address the obligation of colleges and universities under Section 504 for the first time. In this case, Frances Davis, a woman with a hearing disability, had applied to a clinical nursing program at Southeastern Community College, an institution receiving federal funds. Davis brought suit after her application was denied, alleging that she was denied acceptance solely based on her hearing disability (Michigan State University [MSU], 2013). In the suit, Southeastern Community College defended their decision to deny her application, stating that she was not "otherwise qualified" under Section 504 of the Rehabilitation Act because, even if reasonable accommodations were provided, she would still be unable to participate in the training program in a safe and responsible manner. The institution demonstrated that the applicant's ability to understand vocal speech without relying on lip reading was a necessary component of ensuring safety for the patients a nurse works with in the field.

The Court "determined that an otherwise qualified handicapped individual protected by Section 504 is one who is qualified *in spite of* his or her disability, and thus ruled that the institution need not make major program modifications to accommodate the individual" (Kaplin & Lee, 2007, p. 154). The court found that Section 504 only requires that a person with a disability not be denied the benefits of a postsecondary program solely on the basis of his or her disability (MSU, 2013). Since Davis could not be admitted to the nursing program without substantial admission and programmatic requirement changes, her denied application did not constitute discrimination by the institution. Thus, the court established that technical standards for admission were permissible. This case established the early definition of "otherwise qualified" under Section 504 (Hurley, 1991, p. 1063).

Pushkin v. Regents of the University of Colorado (1981)

The next case, *Pushkin v. Regents of the University of Colorado* (1981), clarified the burden of proof in discrimination suits brought under Section 504 of the Rehabilitation Act. In *Pushkin*, the plaintiff was a medical doctor with multiple sclerosis who had been denied admission to the university's psychiatric residency program on the basis of his physical disability. The Admissions committee at the University of Colorado interviewed Dr. Pushkin for 45 minutes and, upon that interaction, denied him admission, stating "that (a) they were concerned how patients would react to Dr. Pushkin; (b) they felt Dr. Pushkin had not come to terms with his disability, and that this would affect his ability to treat patients; (c) Dr. Pushkin would not be able to handle the stress on the job on account of his condition; and (d) Dr. Pushkin would require too much medical care to be able to satisfy the requirements of the job" (Rose, 2013, para. 3). Within the trial, evidence was also presented by medical professionals and Dr. Pushkin himself, supporting his abilities to handle the stress of the job and his ongoing medical treatments. The Court found that Dr. Pushkin was in fact discriminated against by the institution.

The rationale in the *Pushkin* case provided clear support for an individualized review of each applicant and established a precedent that institutions must not stereotype people with disabilities when reviewing their qualifications for certain programs. The *Pushkin* case set forth guidelines for determining whether an applicant is "otherwise qualified" for admission, regardless of their disability. The court outlined that first and foremost, it is the plaintiff's burden to show that he or she was otherwise qualified for the program apart from his or her disability and that the rejection was based exclusively on the disability. Second, to dispute this, the institution must prove that the applicant's rejection was for reasons other than his or her disability. Finally, the plaintiff must show rebuttal evidence demonstrating that the institution's reasoning for rejecting him or her was based on unfounded or stereotyping conclusions of disability (Kaplin & Lee, 2007).

Doe v. New York University (1981)

The next case, *Doe v. New York University* (1981), used the precedent and burden of proof established in the *Pushkin* case to find in favor of the plaintiff, Jane Doe. Doe was a medical student at New York University (NYU) who had a history of borderline personality disorder (BPD). Upon completing a physical examination as part of the entrance requirements for all first-year students, the examining doctor noticed scars on Doe's body that were indicative of self-harm. On her application for admission, Doe had stated that she did not have any chronic or recurrent illnesses or emotional problems; however, after the physical examination, she acknowledged her history of BPD. NYU initially recommended that she withdraw from the university, but eventually allowed her to continue in the program with the understanding that she receive psychiatric therapy. The institution also warned her that if she had further psychiatric issues, she would be expected to withdraw from medical school. Soon after, Doe inflicted physical harm upon herself as a means of dealing with stress, and the institution put her on a leave of absence, during which she underwent treatment in California (Liebert, 2003).

The following year, Doe applied for readmission to NYU's medical school, but her request was denied. The university asserted that Doe would not be able to fully overcome BPD and that it would only be a matter of time before she experienced another psychiatric issue. Doe sought legal intervention, claiming she was discriminated against based on her disability and that this discrimination was in direct violation of Section 504 of the Rehabilitation Act. The Judge found in favor of Jane Doe, stating that she was, in fact, denied readmission based on her disability. She was reinstated to NYU's medical school in 1981, and went on to complete a graduate degree at Harvard and work for the Department of Education and Welfare (Liebert, 2003).

Doherty v. Southern College of Optometry (1988)

Following the *Southeastern Community College v. Davis* case in 1979, courts began inquiring into reasonable accommodations in order to determine whether or not a student with a disability is "otherwise qualified." The case of *Doherty v. Southern College of Optometry* (1988) looked closer into this issue. The plaintiff, James Paul Doherty, had retinitis pigmentosa, an eye disease resulting in loss of peripheral vision and poor vision in low-light environments, as well as a neurological condition impacting his motor skills and coordination. After he began attending Southern, the school changed the curriculum to include a clinical proficiency test requirement, where each student must perform certain techniques in an exam-room setting. Doherty failed this clinical exam because of his disability, and as a result, the institution refused to confer his degree. Doherty alleged that "deviations from the stated curriculum breached his contractual rights" (Kaplin & Lee, 2007, p. 298). However, the school handbook included language reserving the right to alter degree requirements, and had done so in years prior to Doherty's attendance. This portion of the plaintiff's claim was dismissed, and the court ruled that the curricular changes were reasonable.

In addition, the *Doherty* court "considered the relationship between Section 504's 'otherwise qualified' requirement and the institution's duty to provide a 'reasonable accommodation' for a student with a disability" (Kaplin & Lee, 2007, p. 332). The court held that an "otherwise qualified" person with a disability is someone "who, with the aid of reasonable modifications by the school, meets the required standards of the school's program" (Hurley, 1991, pp. 1065–1066). This decision established new precedent over the *Davis* case, which stipulated that a student with a disability must be able to meet all of a school's requirements *despite* their disabilities. As a result of the *Doherty* case, the court established a balancing approach used to determine whether a student with a disability is "otherwise qualified" under Section 504.

Wynne v. Tufts University School of Medicine (1992)

Steven Wynne, a former student of Tufts University School of Medicine, brought suit against the institution in this case (*Wynne v. Tufts University School of Medicine*, 1992). Wynne was a medical school student with a learning disability who was dismissed from the program on academic grounds after failing repeated courses and exams. Wynne alleged that he was discriminated against due to his disability after he had requested that Tufts refrain from using multiple-choice exams as an accommodation. Upon hearing the case, the court initially agreed with Wynne, but when the matter came back on appeal, the Court "accepted Tufts' explanation that critical thinking skills were taught by use of multiple-choice exams and therefore allowed the dismissal of the case" (Rose, 2013, para. 5).

In the *Wynne* case, the university provided far-reaching evidence of their attempts to accommodate Wynne. For example, the institution paid for his neuropsychological testing, allowed him to repeat his first year of medical school, permitted him to re-take tests, and made note-takers and tutors available to him (Kaplin & Lee, 2007). Because of this extensive evidence of multiple forms of assistance that were offered to Wynne, the court was satisfied that the school met all requirements established in Section 504 of the Rehabilitation Act, despite the school's inflexible stance on multiple-choice exams. The *Wynne* case delineated that institutions should "show that (a) officials with relevant duties and experiences considered the accommodation request; (b) that they meaningfully considered the impact on the program and the availability of alternatives; and (c) that they reached a rational conclusion that accommodations could not be offered" (Rose, 2013, para. 6).

Guckenberger v. Boston University (1997–1998)

Guckenberger v. Boston University was a three-part case in 1997–1998 that resulted in several lengthy decisions that significantly helped shape the disability discrimination landscape in the courts. In the first part of this case (*Guckenberger v. Boston University*, 957 F. Supp. 306, D. Mass., 1997), students at Boston University (BU) claimed the institution was in violation of nondiscrimination laws when they implemented a new policy requiring students to provide recent documentation of learning disabilities. The policy required this documentation be dated within the last three years. The students also challenged the evaluation and appeal process for the request of academic accommodations, as well as the prohibition against math and foreign language course substitutions. Finally, the students felt that the university president had created a "hostile environment" when he made negative comments about students with learning disabilities (Kaplin & Lee, 2007). The court found that the plaintiffs' claim of a hostile environment fell short of reprimand under the law, but did grant class action certification for the plaintiffs on their other challenges.

In the second part of the case (*Guckenberger v. Boston University*, 974 F. Supp. 106, D. Mass., 1997), the district court addressed some of the issues students brought forth about the requirement that testing needed to occur within the last three years, as well as the institution's inflexible stance on math and foreign language course substitutions. The court pointed out that the institution had altered some of their policies after the litigation began, and that the majority of these alterations appeased the court's initial review that the university had violated the ADA and Section 504. The court found that documentation of a learning disability did not need to take place every three years, unless medically necessary. The court ruled that various professionals could screen individuals for learning disabilities, and not just individuals with doctorates, as the university had originally stipulated. Finally, the court's decision found that the university's choice to change a policy in the middle of an academic year without proper notice given to students was a violation of the ADA and Section 504. In addition, the court noted that "the president and his staff lacked experience or expertise in diagnosing learning disabilities or in fashioning appropriate accommodations had personally administered the policy on the basis of uninformed stereotypes about the learning disabled" (Kaplin & Lee, 2007, p. 451).

In the third part of this case (*Guckenberger v. Boston University*, 8 F. Supp. 2d 82, D. Mass., 1998), the court addressed the issues brought forth regarding inflexible course substitution at BU. The plaintiffs had claimed they were discriminated against when the institution would not approve course substitutions for students with learning disabilities, as was customary in previous years. The court ruled that, if BU could establish a "deliberative process" demonstrating that course substitutes would lower academic standards at the institution and/or significantly alter the program of study, then it could refuse course substitutions for students with learning disabilities (Rose, 2013). This case relied on the deliberative process outlined in the *Wynne* case, and the court was satisfied with the university's justification of not accepting substitute courses as an accommodation.

University of Alabama v. Garrett (2001)

In *University of Alabama v. Garrett* (2001), two state employees brought suit against their Alabama state employers, seeking monetary damages under Title I of the Americans with Disabilities Act. Patricia Garrett was the director of Nursing for the University of Alabama. When her breast cancer diagnoses caused her to take substantial leave time from work, her supervisor informed her that she would need to sacrifice her position at the institution. Milton Ash was a security officer at the Alabama Department of Youth Services. Ash requested his job duties be modified to accommodate his chronic asthma, but was denied and ultimately given poor performance evaluations as a result. Both Garrett and Ash felt they had been discriminated against due to their disabilities. This case called into question an individual's ability to sue a state for damages under the Americans with Disabilities Act. The United States Supreme Court heard the case, and ruled that "employment provisions of the ADA are subject to Eleventh Amendment immunity...this means that public institutions cannot be sued for money damages under the ADA for alleged employment discrimination in federal court" (Kaplin & Lee, 2007, pp. 446–447).

Conclusion

A discussion of the Disability Movement in the United States begins in this monograph by defining disability according to the two major pieces of legislation: Section 504 of the Rehabilitation Act and the Americans with Disabilities Act. According to Section 504, individuals with disabilities are defined as "persons with a physical or mental impairment which substantially limits one or more major life activities. Major life activities include caring for one's self, walking, seeing, hearing, speaking, breathing, working, performing manual tasks, and learning" (United States Department of Health and Human Services, 2006, para. 3). And, according to the Americans with Disabilities Act, an individual is considered to have a disability if "s/he has a physical or mental impairment that substantially limits one or more major life activities, has a record of such an impairment, or is regarded as having such an impairment" (United States Department of Justice, 2002, para. 6). Frequently, individuals define disability based on their own experience, or lack thereof, which sometimes results in a narrow understanding of disability. For the purposes of this monograph, disability has a wide-range scope and encompasses physical, mental, and psychological disabilities, which are both visible and invisible to others.

Early pieces of legislation in the Disability Movement and the Disability Movement's relationship to the Civil Rights and Women's Rights Movements were addressed in this chapter. One of the earliest accounts of the United States assisting people with disabilities was when President Lincoln established funding for Washington DC's Gallaudet University, a school for deaf students, in the 1860s. Since that time, major policies such as the Civil Rights

Act and Title IX have helped pave the way for disability legislation to be enacted. Two of the most prolific acts outlining the rights and responsibilities of Americans with disabilities, as well as establishing benchmarks for nondiscrimination and accessibility, are Section 504 of the Rehabilitation Act, passed in 1973, and the Americans with Disabilities Act, passed in 1990. These two pieces of legislation continue to protect people with disabilities today.

The chapter addressed seven important court cases that established precedence in the legal system for people with disabilities seeking recourse under the law. Dating back to *Southeastern Community College v. Davis* in 1979 and continuing through *University of Alabama v. Garrett* in 2001, these seven court cases were instrumental in helping outline the ways in which colleges and universities needed to work with people with disabilities. Unresolved issues remain, however, which the courts will continue to address in the years to come as more students with disabilities enter the nation's colleges and universities.

Disability of College Campuses: An Overview

> I am an invisible man. I am a man of substance, of flesh and bone, fiber and liquids—and I might even be said to possess a mind. I am invisible, understand, simply because people refuse to see me.
>
> Ralph Ellison (1952, p. 3)

SIMILAR TO ELLISON'S "INVISIBLE MAN" (a racial reference), students with disabilities may feel invisible on college campuses. In the video *Uncertain Welcome* (General College, University of Minnesota, 2002), college students express concerns about disclosing their disabilities to faculty. The fear of stigma, discrimination, and segregation is articulated, and even the fear of retaliation if they "push too hard" for an accommodation is conveyed. Although some of the students in the video describe positive experiences with professors who readily offer their assistance with the accommodation process, the fact that students are fearful to disclose their disabilities on college campuses is a concern that should be addressed. In order for students with documented disabilities to feel comfortable with "the system" and confident they will receive the necessary accommodations, it is the shared responsibility of educators and professionals to provide safe, secure, and welcoming environments. An institution's mission should not only be to follow the letter of the law but also to embrace and demonstrate the spirit of the law through how students are treated on a daily basis.

This chapter provided an overview of the status of disability in United States higher education. Key arenas for examining disability, including access and climate, are elaborated. An analysis of who is on campus is explored, including disability statistics, types of disabilities, and a brief discussion of disability accommodations and services.

Disability in Higher Education: What Is It?

Disability in higher education includes an institution's students and employees with disabilities, the college or university's Disability Services offices, the process of arranging for accommodations for students and employees with disabilities, and any cocurricular or curricular learning opportunities related to the topic of disability. Some institutions have an entire academic department devoted to disability studies, while other institutions have a class or two throughout their course offerings. On the cocurricular side, some institutions have a plethora of learning opportunities available to students, while others may or may not even include disability in conversations of diversity or multicultural education. Diversity and multicultural education itself is commonplace on college campuses, but disability is sometimes not included as an aspect of diversity.

How are students with disabilities similar and different from students in other "minority" groups? Gallardo and Gibson (2005) emphasize the similarities between disability identity and racial identity when they compare Gibson's Identity Development Model with Sue and Sue's (2008) Racial/Cultural Identity Development Model. Both groups tend to move from a type of passive awareness/conformity phase and potentially through an acceptance phase, similar to identity development of gay and lesbian individuals according to Fassinger's (1998) identity model. It is common for higher education institutions to group students of various "minority" populations together when assuring the protection of these marginalized students. However, the authors of this monograph encourage college professionals to intentionally discuss and determine why all of these students are viewed as "one" and what pitfalls occur as a result of viewing them all together.

Tregoning (2009) refers to "in-group" and "out-of-group" circumstances related to disabilities. Some students with disabilities may not see themselves as members of marginalized populations. Many do not see or choose not to see themselves similar to other students with disabilities (Getzel & Briel, 2006; Getzel & McManus, 2005), particularly when it comes to categorizing disabilities. For example, students with learning disabilities may not choose to identify with students with visual or mobility disabilities. Most see themselves as students who learn differently than other students (Wieland, 2009); they do not view themselves as similar to students who need accessible facilities and assistive aids. Massie-Burrell (2009), a woman with a congenital limb amputation, identifies herself in this way:

> I am an African American woman with a disability—a circumstance that places me in the "multiple oppressions" category. I prefer to use the phrase "multiple identities" because who I am is the intersection of race, gender, and disability among other social identities that I claim . . . Individuals are much more than their disability . . . Some prefer to be left alone and view their disability as a mere inconvenience, while others "claim" it (Linton, 1998). We all are very different; the same disability can yield a variety of outcomes. (p. 60)

Some students with disabilities, however, may see a connection to other students with disabilities. When discussing his "unexpected additional identity" (i.e., Human Immunodeficiency Virus, HIV), McDonald-Dennis (2009) describes his first meeting with the Standing Committee on Disability in ACPA College Student Educators International:

> I was afraid I did not belong. I saw people in wheelchairs, others signing, and some with canes. I assumed these were the "true" people with disabilities and I was an imposter. To my surprise, no one accused me of being fake . . . I was overjoyed as I spoke to others who had disabilities, which were different from mine, yet were able to

speak about the marginalization, the joys we have in our lives, and
what it means to be a person with a disability. (p. 68)

Pederson's (1988) Multicultural Development Model, focusing on awareness, knowledge, and skills, provides a framework for disability education (Evans, Herriott, & Myers, 2009). According to Pederson (1988), multicultural awareness includes values, attitudes, and assumptions needed to work with diverse populations; multicultural knowledge is the information about a particular population; and multicultural skills are behaviors needed to apply awareness and skills to specific situations. Although disability is often omitted from diversity education or is included as an afterthought (Palombi, 2000), applying Pederson's model is an effective approach to disability education and its inclusion in multicultural development.

A large part of disability education is acquiring the knowledge of disability law (outlined in the previous chapter) and reasonable accommodations. Providing accommodations to students with disabilities at colleges and universities occurred primarily after the passage of the Rehabilitation Act of 1973 (Public Law 93–112, 1973). Section 504 of that act specifically stated that all federally funded postsecondary education institutions could not discriminate against persons with disabilities, and therefore, accommodations should be provided to those qualified students in order to "level the playing field." The guidelines for this law were not disseminated until 1977, and, even then, many postsecondary educational institutions did not comply. As students were not receiving accommodations, litigation began. The Office of Civil Rights (OCR) investigated a multitude of complaints regarding disability discrimination. Cases were heard in district courts; some were settled out of court while others moved to appellate courts. Some cases were brought before the Supreme Court, such as those listed in the second chapter, focusing specifically on the definition of disability and the issues of "reasonable accommodations," "otherwise qualified," "mitigating circumstances," and "fundamentally altered." With a need to expand the law to prohibit discrimination on the basis of disabilities in nonfederally funded educational institutions, Congress passed The Americans with Disabilities Act (ADA) of 1990 (Public Law 101–336, 1990), civil rights legislation designed to protect the rights of all people with disabilities in the areas of employment, public accommodations, state and local government, and telecommunication. This applied to all public and private colleges and universities' employment, services, programs, and activities.

With the passage of the ADA came mandated training on college campuses. As a result, more institutions developed formalized processes for providing accommodations and services to students with disabilities. The number of disability services providers, offices, and centers grew on college campuses and accountability measures were put into place where few had previously existed. The accommodation process, including the type of documentation required and how documentation would be verified, was developed and fine-tuned throughout the country (Brinckerhoff, Shaw, & McGuire, 1992). The Association for Higher Education and Disability (AHEAD, 2012) was a leader in developing guidelines for disability services providers and the accommodation process. In 1979, the Council for the Advancement of Standards (CAS) in Higher Education began to develop standards for functional areas in postsecondary institutions, including disability services and resources. Using 12 guiding criteria "to promote the improvement of programs and services to enhance the quality of student learning and development" (CAS, 2012, para. 2), disability services providers and college administrators were provided with guidance for enhancing current programs and creating new initiatives to improve disability services and promote inclusion on their campuses. Currently, Disability Resources and Services are one of 43 functional areas addressed in the CAS Standards.

College Students With Disabilities: Who Are They?

Statistics on disability vary depending on the source. The United States Census, for example, does not use the same definition of disability as does the federal government and its legislations (Brault, 2012). The United States Census asks individuals whether or not they experience specific functional limitations (e.g., use a cane, wheelchair, crutches; have difficulty walking a half mile; have a learning disability; are blind, etc.). According to these self-reports, "approximately 56.7 million people (18.7%) of the 303.9 million in the civilian noninstitutionalized population had a disability in 2010" (Brault, 2012, p. 4). In reference to higher education, statistics show that approximately 11% of college students have reported a diagnosed and documented disability (ED NCES, 2012a):

> *Much of the growth between 2000 and 2010 was in full-time enrollment; the number of full-time students rose 45 percent, while the number of part-time students rose 26 percent. During the same time period, the number of females rose 39 percent, while the number of males rose 35 percent. Enrollment increases can be affected both by population growth and by rising rates of enrollment. (ED NCES, 2012a, Chapter 3, para. 3)*

Here is a snapshot demographic profile of students with disabilities in postsecondary institutions during the 2007–2008 academic year from the United States Department of Education National Center for Educational Statistics (NCES):

> *In 2007–08, the percentages of undergraduates who were male (43%) and female (57%) were the same for undergraduates reporting disabilities as for those not reporting disabilities. There were some differences in characteristics such as race/ethnicity, age, dependency status, and veteran status between undergraduates reporting disabilities and those without disabilities in 2007–08. For example, White students made up a larger percentage of undergraduates reporting disabilities than of undergraduates without disabilities (66% vs. 62%). Undergraduates under age 24 made up a smaller percentage of those reporting disabilities than of those not reporting disabilities (54% vs. 60%). A smaller percentage of undergraduates who reported disabilities than of those without disabilities were dependents (47% vs. 53%). About 4% of undergraduates who reported disabilities were veterans, compared with 3% of those who did not report disabilities. (ED NCES, 2012a, Chapter 3, para. 3)*

The graduation rate of students with disabilities is approximately 26%, half of the rate of students without disabilities (Gregg, 2009).

Based on results of the Cooperative Institutional Research Program (CIRP) survey, the oldest longitudinal survey on higher education in the United States and cosponsored by the American Council on Education and the Higher Education Research Institute at the University of California Los Angeles (HERI, 2012), first-year students who reported having disabilities listed "business" and "arts and humanities" as their top choice of majors, and, like their peers without disabilities, listed their top career choices as business executive, engineer, elementary school teacher/administrator, and computer programmer and analyst. Compared to students without disabilities, they reported receiving fewer college-based grants, will require more tutoring and remedial services, and will need extra time to complete their degrees. "A smaller share of [first-year] students with disabilities than other students rated themselves as 'above average or in the top 10% of people' on most measures of self-esteem, academic ability, and physical health" (Henderson, 2001, p. 14). This supports the findings in the next section related to attitudes of students with disabilities.

Learning disability was the fastest growing disability reported by first-year students between 1988 and 2000 (Henderson, 2001). "By 2000, two in five [first-year students] with disabilities (40%) cited a learning disability . . . " compared to 16% in 1988 (p. 5). According to several reports (Henderson, 2001; Jarrow, 1993; ED NCES, 2012a, 2012b), ADD/ADHD and other learning disabilities are the largest disability group on many college campuses. A large percentage of institutions that enrolled students with disabilities during 2008–2009 reported enrolling students with specific learning disabilities (86%) and ADD/ADHD (79%) (ED NCES, 2012a, 2012b).

The number of college students with autism spectrum disorder and psychological disabilities is on the rise at 2% and 15%, respectively (Raue & Lewis, 2011). With growing enrollment of United States military (Miles, 2010) using the Post-9/11 GI Bill (Grossman, 2009), the number of students with post-traumatic stress disorder (PTSD) is increasing. Based on national figures, 40 million people have been diagnosed with some type of anxiety disorder, and over seven million specifically have PTSD (National Institute of Mental Health [NIMH], 2013). According to Wilson (1988), a large percentage of veterans do not disclose having PTSD to educational institutions for fear of being stigmatized. Percentage distribution of types of disabilities reported by two-year and four-year degree-granting postsecondary institutions that enrolled students with disabilities in 2008–2009 were as follows: hearing 4%; seeing 3%; speaking 1%; mobility or orthopedic 7%; Traumatic Brain Injury 2%; specific learning disabilities 31%; ADD/ADHD 18%; autism spectrum disorder 2%; cognitive or intellectual disabilities 3%; health including chronic conditions 11%; mental illness, psychological, or psychiatric conditions 15%; and other 3% (Raue & Lewis, 2011, Table 4).

In the same report by the United States Department of Education (Raue & Lewis, 2011), 88% of two-year and four-year Title IV (those receiving federal student financial aid) eligible degree-granting postsecondary institutions reported enrolling students with disabilities during the 2008–2009 academic year, and "almost all public two-year and four-year institutions (99%) and medium and large institutions (100%) reported enrolling students with disabilities" (p. 3). With this growth in enrollment comes the continued and pressing need for further research and scholarship regarding college students with disabilities (Snyder & Dillow, 2010).

College Students With Disabilities: What Are They Saying?

College students with disabilities experience challenges similar to their peers without disabilities. However, according to some studies (Cohen, 2004; M. Sandler, 2008), students with disabilities may experience even more anxiety and overwhelming feelings during their transition from high school to college than their peers without disabilities. As previously noted, students with disabilities have lower retention rates (particularly during the first two years of college) than their counterparts without disabilities (Gregg, 2009).

It is common to see studies in the area of disability research that do not include the voices of people with disabilities; instead, they are often *about* people with disabilities or report attitudes of persons without disabilities toward those with disabilities. During the past 20 years, numerous studies focused on the academic and social perspectives of students without disabilities toward individuals with disabilities, examining college major, year in college, gender, and level of contact with students with disabilities (e.g., Fichten, 1986; Lyons & Hayes, 1993; Upton et al., 2005; Yuker, 1994; among others). In a recent study conducted by Meyer et al. (2012) on attitudes of students without disabilities toward students with learning disabilities and their accommodations, students from public and private institutions responded revealing few negative attitudes. Most paid little attention to the accommodations received by other students and did not discuss the topic of accommodations with other students. In response to an open-ended question, one student expressed what seemed to be a common reaction among the respondents:

> *In general, I do not think college students care about what accommodations are given to students with LD and ADD. I would say the average student does not even know who has learning disabilities in his or her classroom. I would not consider it to be a large problem in the college setting. Students have themselves to worry about. (Meyer et al., 2012, p. 178)*

In a study by Getzel and Thoma (2008), students with disabilities at the postsecondary level identified self-determination as a key factor for their success. For some students with disabilities, the idea of a fresh start may have a negative influence. In many instances, these students may see college as a way to break away from their disability. Disclosing their disability to the university may conflict with the student's desire to have a new beginning, one in which they do not feel labeled by their peers and faculty (Getzel & Briel, 2006; Getzel & McManus, 2005). Without self-determination, students with disabilities often become frustrated by the new set of challenges they face on campus. Students with disabilities must adapt to managing their academics while also being responsible for requesting accommodations, providing appropriate documentation in order to receive the accommodations, and creating relationships with faculty to ensure the support they need is implemented (Getzel & Thoma, 2008).

Too often, the focus on students with disabilities relates only to academic accommodations. However, higher education professionals must focus on the holistic growth of all of our students. A study by Sachs and Schreuer (2011) shows that academic achievements and overall experiences of students with and without disabilities were somewhat similar, but a real difference was in social inclusion and involvement in extracurricular activities between these same groups. In the academic differences that do exist for students with and without disabilities, it appears that accessibility, not ability, is to blame. Students with disabilities may find it more difficult to meet the requirements embedded in Western culture. Western society values time and frequently measures productivity and achievement by high-speed completion of tasks (Lerner et al., 2003). These high-speed time constraints may prove difficult for students who do not receive proper accommodations.

Creative approaches to accommodations must be taken in order to improve the campus environment for students with disabilities. More flexible admission procedures provide greater opportunities for students with disabilities to enter institutions of higher learning. However, without breaking down current barriers at the institutional level, they may be set up to fail far before they enter the classroom. Institutions must go beyond the simple accommodation of extra exam time by providing innovative resources for students with disabilities (Sachs & Schreuer, 2011).

Providing well-designed opportunities for students with disabilities to become more acquainted with campus is a step in the right direction; however, institutions must also move to create social change in their campus communities. The perception of students with disabilities must change in those individuals who do not identify with a disability. The attitudes faculty and peers have toward students with disabilities greatly influence the students' college experience. Institutions must advocate for social change by providing learning opportunities about disabilities. Through awareness, a campus' culture and climate toward students with disabilities will improve (Myers, 2009a).

In a recent study, students with disabilities were asked what advocacy skills were essential to their retention in college. Four strong themes emerged from the discussion. The students indicated "seeking services from DSS ... and college services available to all students; forming relationships with professors and instructors; developing support systems on campus with friends, support groups, and … DSS office; and gaining a self-awareness of understanding of themselves to persevere" (Getzel & Thoma, 2008, p. 81) were vital to their success at the postsecondary level. Self-advocacy was a large component of their success, but it did not come easy. Many of the students had to become more self-aware in order to understand their strengths and weaknesses. Only after they had delved further into understanding their own disability were they able to become better advocates for themselves. These students indicated they learned by trial and error, but also agreed that it would be preferable if identity-development efforts began earlier in their college experience (Getzel & Thoma, 2008).

Teaching students with disabilities self-advocacy skills is essential (McCarthy, 2007). It may benefit institutions to host short-term opportunities for students prior to the start of the semester to help them learn applicable skills for navigating their future environments. Landmark College is at the forefront of this endeavor for students with learning disabilities. Landmark currently operates boot camp programs each summer, which help students to build on their strengths and learn to advocate for themselves (Marklein, 2011). The knowledge and guidance these students receive can help them acclimate to their campus and make them feel more comfortable in their new environment. In turn, such training might even lead to higher retention rates among students with disabilities.

Perceptions and Preferences of Students and Employees With Disabilities

College and university students and employees with disabilities have relatively similar expectations for campus ecology (Strange & Banning, 2001). Myers and Bastian (2010) conducted a research study focused on 35 persons between the ages of 19 and 70 enrolled in institutions of higher education who self-identified as having a visual disability. Three main themes emerged from the study for expectations of the college environment. The first theme, respect, focused on the behavior of others who did not have a visual impairment. Participants wanted to avoid being prejudged, and wanted to be treated with courtesy and experience effective communication. When interacting with faculty, participants were strong believers in self-advocacy but expressed the need to establish positive rapport with faculty. Respondents also addressed inappropriate behavior for respect. Largely inappropriate behaviors included either a lack of knowledge or a lack of common deference for others, including grabbing people, petting guide dogs, and rude comments being made to the person with a visual disability. The second theme, of comfort, addressed the idea of the person with the visual disability making others feel comfortable through initiating conversation or making a joke. Participants also reflected on not being comfortable with themselves and how that impacts positive interactions with others. The final theme, of awareness, reflected on ideas such as disability awareness training for others to develop stronger communication skills to work with students with disabilities. Additionally, participants suggested implementing UID principles to ensure access, create inclusive environments, and therefore eliminate feelings of isolation.

To assist with perceptions and awareness of students with disabilities, one strategy that should be implemented is social norming for disability. As stated in Myers et al. (2009), "social norming focuses on the positive outcomes rather than negative behaviors" (para. 2). Social norming assists students to align their inflated perceptions with the actual reality of the issue at hand. If students believe there is a negative attitude toward individuals with disabilities on campus, one might be more inclined to collude with negative actions if observed due to the inflated perception that others believe and act the same way. Aligning the factual, evidence-based attitudes and behaviors with students' perceptions will then allow personal actions to align in a more informed and authentic manner. In this example, a student would be more likely to intervene and speak, as an ally to a person with a disability, if they know the campus is largely uncomfortable witnessing prejudice.

Campus climate has a large role in the successes of students and employees with disabilities. An area of challenge for higher education beyond climate is to provide work place accommodations. Conversations on disability largely focus on students with disabilities, providing needed accommodations for their curricular and cocurricular lives. However, it is important to ensure that employment opportunities for students, faculty, and staff are also providing a necessary level of accessibility. Employers at an institution should consider flexible hours, restructuring a position, facilities and technology accessibility, and modifying equipment or materials (Reilly & Davis, 2005) to provide accommodations for a person with a disability. When speaking about accessibility for employment, however, the conversation typically only revolves around physical approachability. A necessary conversation must occur about accessibility of employment for people with learning disabilities and how to examine positions through this lens as well.

Disability Services in Higher Education: What Is Provided?

Over 20 years ago, Brinckerhoff et al. (1992) identified several areas in higher education that might affect outcomes for college students with learning disabilities. Their focused areas, including the difference between high school and college settings, the determination of legibility and access, the determination of reasonable accommodations, and the fostering of independence and self-advocacy, continue to be the focus of disability service providers today. This is evident in the work of Getzel and Thoma (2008), Myers and Bastian (2010), and Marklein (2011) relating to students with disabilities, in Franke, Bérubé, O'Neil, and Kurland's (2012) research on accommodating faculty with disabilities, and in the scholarship of Higbee and Mitchell (2009) regarding student affairs professionals with disabilities.

A survey at a large Midwest research institution regarding faculty knowledge, attitudes, and practices related to students with disabilities revealed almost half of the respondents had limited interaction with students with disabilities, limited knowledge regarding accommodations, no training in disability, and little knowledge of disability law. The faculty, however, did have more teaching experience with students with learning disabilities than with students with other disabilities (Leyser, Vogel, Wyland, & Brulle, 1998). Compared to a study at the same institution 10 years prior, the results varied. Faculty in the earlier study had less disability training, and their teaching experience was with students with visual, hearing, and psychiatric disabilities (Leyser, 1989), thus indicating the enrollment growth of students with learning disabilities and the increase in disability education. In a study of administrators in the California Community College system, Guillermo (2003) found respondents were aware of the need to accommodate students but were less informed about their institution's process for obtaining the accommodations. In addition, a lack of understanding of the "institution's commitment to barrier-free access to learning as well as the overall physical accessibility of the campus was evident" (Guillermo, 2003, p. 4). In a 2008 national study of graduate students in higher education administration programs, over half of the respondents reported that they do not know what steps to take to ensure that students with disabilities can fully participate in higher education, and almost three fourths of the respondents saw a need for a disability awareness course in their curriculum (Myers, 2008a). Considering these studies span two decades, it is clear that there is a continued interest in and need for some type of disability education.

The results of the NCES study on students with disabilities at two-year and four-year Title IV–eligible degree-granting postsecondary institutions during 2008–2009 provide useful information regarding the current state of affairs relative to disability services; documentation verification; accommodations provided; disability knowledge, education, and training; and the use of universal design. Below is a paraphrased summary of the featured findings provided by the ED NCES (2012a):

- *Accommodations*: 83% provided additional exam time as an accommodation to students with disabilities. Large percentages provided classroom note takers, faculty-provided written course notes or assignments, help with learning strategies or study skills alternative exam formats, and adaptive equipment and technology.
- *Documentation*: 92% required verification of disability, some accepted Individualized Education Program (IEP) and 504 Plan from secondary school, while 80% accepted a comprehensive vocational rehabilitation agency evaluation.

- *Communication with students*: 79% distributed materials designed to encourage students with disabilities to identify themselves to the institution.
- *Communication with faculty and staff*: 92% provided one-on-one discussions when requested to assist faculty and staff in working with students with disabilities.
- *Website accessibility*: 93% used a main website to post information about the institution. One fourth of those reported the institution's main website follows established accessibility guidelines or recommendations for users with disabilities to a major extent.
- *Campus accessibility*: 89% integrated accessibility features during major renovation and new construction projects, most offered students, faculty, and staff the opportunity to provide input on accessibility features during project planning stages, and most conducted needs assessments pertaining to accessibility (64%).
- *Services for the public*: 35% provided various services and accommodations to the general public, for example, publicizing the availability of adaptive equipment, technology, or services at institution-sponsored events open to the public.
- *UD barriers*: Barriers hindering implementation of universal design to a moderate or major extent were limited staff resources to provide faculty and staff training on accessibility issues (52%), costs associated with purchasing appropriate technology (46%), and other institutional priorities (45%) (Raue & Lewis, 2011, pp. 3–4).

These findings confirm that institutions of higher education are taking appropriate steps to ensure equal access to students with disabilities and provide respectful, welcoming environments. Although some may continue to hold on to the myths and misperceptions related to people with disabilities, including the idea that accommodations are cost-prohibitive, evidence to the contrary exists (Unger, 2002; Wells, 2001). Changing attitudes is one of the most important keys to improving the status of students with disabilities. Through professional development initiatives, improved websites, intentional communication, and utilization of universal design, institutions are on the right track to inclusion.

Students With Disabilities: A Shared Responsibility

Providing accessible learning environments both inside and outside of the classroom is a shared responsibility (Bryan & Myers, 2006). It is common for members of the campus community to assume that students with disabilities are the responsibility of the Disability Services office given the fact that, at most institutions, Disability Services verifies disability documentation and "assigns" reasonable accommodations. Best practices, however, encourage us to shift that paradigm. To borrow the phrase, "it takes a village . . . ," it really does take the entire higher education community to ensure the success of its students—*all* of its students—including those with disabilities. Negative or misguided attitudes toward students with disabilities must be altered, and allies can help set a tone to change those attitudes (Casey-Powell & Souma, 2009; Marks, 1999).

To assist the campus community in ensuring equal access and inclusion, user-friendly resources are available to assist postsecondary disability service providers, faculty, administrators, and staff. Such resources include the Association of Higher Education and Disability (AHEAD), the University of Washington Disabilities, Opportunities, Internetworking, and Technology (DO IT) program, the University of Minnesota's Pedagogy and Student Services for Institutional Transformation (PASS IT) project, California State University Northridge (CSUN) International Technology and Persons with Disabilities Conference, Cornell University's Employment and Disability Institute, and the World Wide Web Consortium (W3C). AHEAD (http://www.ahead.org) offers guidelines for accommodations, publications, and programs in addition to association memberships and conferences. The DO IT website (http://www.washington.edu/doit) offers a multitude of resources, projects, programs, and resources such as "Access College" comprising The Faculty Room, Student Services Conference Room, The Employment Office, The Student Lounge, The Veterans' Center, The Board Room, and the Center for the Design of Universal Education. Funded by a United States Department of Education grant, PASS IT (http://www.cehd.umn.edu/passit) provides free publications and training materials on universal instructional design, including faculty and staff guidebooks outlining specific strategies to put

UID principles into practice. For almost 30 years, CSUN offers the latest information on adaptive, assistive, and accessible technology at its annual international conference (http://www.csun.edu/cod/conference). Cornell University created the Web Accessibility Toolkit (http://www.webaccesstoolkit.org), providing a one-shop stop for equal access to campus web resources.

W3C is an international community that works together to develop protocol and guidelines for web access and long-term growth of the web:

> *W3C standards define an Open Web Platform for application development that has the unprecedented potential to enable developers to build rich interactive experiences, powered by vast data stores, that are available on any device... W3C develops these technical specifications and guidelines through a process designed to maximize consensus about the content of a technical report, to ensure high technical and editorial quality, and to earn endorsement by W3C and the broader community. (World Wide Web Consortium [W3C], 2012, para. 1–2)*

Other web access assistance includes an Information Technology in Education Accessibility Checklist from AccessIT, the National Center on Accessible Information Technology in Education (http://www.washington.edu/accessit/); the Disability and Business Technical Assistance (DBTAC) national website (http://www.adata.org); Web Accessibility in Mind (WebAIM), Utah State University (http://webaim.org/); Web Accessibility Evaluation (WAVE), WebAIM (http://wave.webaim.org); American Foundation for the Blind (http://www.afb.org); and Accessibility Management Platform (AMP; http://amp.ssbbartgroup.com).

These are just some of the many resources available to ensure inclusion in both face-to-face and online settings. Disability education is *for* everyone, *by* everyone. Through collaborative efforts and open communication, an entire campus community has the potential for providing a welcoming, inclusive environment.

Conclusion

Disability in higher education includes an institution's students and employees with disabilities, the institution's Disability Services office, the accommodation process, and any curricular courses or cocurricular programs related to the topic of disability. Although an important aspect of diversity and multicultural education, disability is sometimes not included in conversations, courses, and programs about diversity on college campuses. This chapter explored the status of disability in United States higher education, and discussed access, accommodations, campus climate, disability statistics, and provided an overview of who is on campus. College students with disabilities represent approximately 11% of the overall college student population (ED NCES, 2012a), but just 26% of students with disabilities persist to graduation—a figure half the rate of students without disabilities (Gregg, 2009). This chapter concluded with a discussion of services provided by Disability Services offices and an overview of the importance of creating shared responsibility throughout an institution. Providing accessible learning environments truly is the responsibility of all faculty, staff, and administrators on campus. A holistic, institution-wide approach to support services greatly enhances the college experience for students with disabilities and improves the likelihood they will be successful both in and outside the classroom.

Understanding Campus Complexity: Problems, Challenges, and Marginalization

> Knowing how to create an inclusive environment is a necessary but not sufficient condition for working effectively with students with disabilities. Educators must also understand the students themselves.
>
> Nancy Evans (2008, p. 11)

NOW THAT AN ANALYSIS OF DISABILITY on college campuses and an overview of the historical elements of the disability movement have been reviewed, it is important to take a closer look at some of the theoretical foundations related to disability. Through a review of the latest research and scholarly perspectives in the field of disability, an in-depth examination of the problems and challenges faced by people with disabilities in higher education is considered. Specifically, this chapter discusses elements of disability and campus complexity by taking a closer look at the major models of disability, student development theories related to disability, and attitudes toward disability. It also examines disability services on campuses and discusses military veterans, a growing subpopulation of students with disabilities at our nation's colleges and universities.

Models of Disability

Within society, there exist varying perspectives about people with disabilities and a wide range of underlying beliefs about disability itself. As a way to understand these diverse viewpoints held by society, it is important to examine the historical underpinnings of disability.

According to Griffin and McClintock (1997), "throughout history, disability has been variously viewed as a sign of spiritual depravity, a cause for ridicule, a genetic weakness to be exterminated, something to be hidden away, a source of pity, a community health problem, and a problem to be fixed" (as cited in Evans, 2008, pp. 11–12). In the 1600s, people with disabilities were widely ridiculed and oftentimes became beggars. In the 1800s, it became commonplace for people with disabilities to be institutionalized in hospitals or asylums in order to remain out of the focus of mainstream society. Some states enacted laws that were in place until the early 1900s that "prohibited persons diseased, maimed, mutilated, or in any way deformed so as to be an unsightly or disgusting object from appearing in public" (Griffin & McClintock, 1997, p. 222). This history of "ableism" sheds light on the domination of the nondisabled experience and point of view (Linton, 1998). Ableism is defined as "discrimination in favor of the able-bodied" and also "includes the idea that a person's abilities or characteristics are determined by disability or that people with disabilities as a group are inferior to nondisabled people" (Linton, 1998, p. 9). Linton (1998) describes this oppression as similar to racist or sexist language, yet not as widely understood by the general American public.

It was not until the mid-1950s that people with disabilities were deinstitutionalized and children with disabilities began to attend public schools with other children. It would take an additional 20 years and a major campaign by people with disabilities to establish equal rights and gain control over their own lives (Evans, 2008). The first key piece of legislation, which was discussed in greater detail in the second chapter, came in the form of 1973's Rehabilitation Act, which prohibited discriminating against people with disabilities. This law was further expanded upon in 1990's Americans with Disabilities Act.

Several major models or frameworks of disability have been prevalent in the United States during different periods of time. These perspectives continue to evolve, and it is important to understand this evolution as a way to make sense of the struggles and challenges people with disabilities continue to face in today's society. These models include the moral model, the medical model, the functional limitations framework, the minority group paradigm, the social construction model, and the social justice perspective.

In her 1996 article, "Toward Inclusive Theory: Disability as Social Construction," Susan Jones defines frameworks through which disability is defined and viewed and through which students with disabilities are understood. Despite the number of years since the article's publication and the advancement in the disability movement during that time, Jones's article continues to be used to describe how disability is perceived by colleges and universities (Higbee & Mitchell, 2009). Descriptions of the disability models follow.

The moral model of disability relates to the attitude that people are morally responsible for their own disabilities because of parent's actions, sin, and bad karma (Mackelprang & Salsgiver, 1999). Some believe disabilities bring spiritual and psychic powers (Griffin & McClintock, 1997). From Hitler's "mercy killings" to euthanasia in nursing homes, people with disabilities, including children, have been and continue to be euthanized because of beliefs that disability is caused by demons and will not result in a quality life. The moral model was demonstrated in the exploitation of people with disabilities in "freak show" and the public's reaction to people with HIV and AIDS.

The medical model of disability views people with disabilities in a pathological sense, seeking a "cure" for their disabilities. In this model, "disability has been understood as a sickness, and disabled people have been understood as invalids" (Hughes, 2002, p. 58). Dominating society's view of disability since the 1700s, the medical model gives control to doctors, service providers, and caretakers, and focuses on what people with disabilities *cannot* do (Michalko, 2002). People with disabilities are seen as medical conditions to be treated (Fine & Asch, 2000) and would not be viable candidates for higher education nor accepted in the college community.

The functional limitations model justifies the status quo, viewing and maintaining the student with a disability in a position of weakness. It focuses on the individual and the individual's "disabling" condition with emphasis on rehabilitation and "fixing" the problem. With the biological reality of disability at the core (Hahn, 1991), this model underscores that the disability is the root of one's problems. It assumes "the pathological and physiological conditions are the primary obstacle to people with disabilities' social integration" (Longmore, 2003, p. 1). Emphasizing deficits and differences, it isolates, marginalizes, and alienates students, affecting sense of self. Perceiving people with disabilities as victims, it leaves the student in need of assistance and support (Fine & Asch, 1988), placing the onus of change on the student rather than on the "disabling" environment. There remains an overriding sense of disability as an individual matter requiring individual attention (Michalko, 2002, p. 161). Examples of the functional limitations model are abundant in research and service within the medical and rehabilitation fields.

The minority group paradigm builds on the "deficit" model, perpetuating myths and stereotypes. The students are members of a minority group (i.e., students with disabilities) and believe they have common social experiences with others in the group. They must have minority group identification and consciousness in this model; however, it is possible that many students with disabilities might not have a connection to others with disabilities or appropriate accommodations for this to occur (Hahn, 1988; Higbee & Mitchell, 2009). With this paradigm come discrimination, alienation, and oppression. Understanding students with disabilities might not occur without considering the results of group status, privilege, and the environment. Advancing beyond the medical model, the minority model acknowledges environmental factors and psychological and social consequences of disability, as well as power structure, discrimination, and group identification as "different" (Scheer, 1994). Jones (1996) purports this model is better than the functional limitations model because it "acknowledges social and psychological consequences of disability . . . [although] neither perspective appropriately acknowledges experiences of the student living with a disability or grapples with the complex interaction of factors that have an impact on those with and those without disability" (p. 350). Examples of the minority group model include disability student organizations, student activists, and students in disability communities and subcultures.

The social construction of disability originated from the work of Asch (1984) and Asch and Fine (1988). This model requires an analysis of people with disabilities and people without disabilities. Most beliefs about disability come from meanings expressed by people without disabilities based on their perceptions, assumptions, and what they have learned. As historian Longmore (2003) purports, "most of the reigning social thought about disability is distorted . . . [and] most of the conventional wisdom about persons with disabilities is wrong" (p. 14). The social construction of disability challenges those assumptions, celebrating the uniqueness of individual differences while focusing on social change and transforming oppressive structures (Asch & Fine, 1988; Jones, 1996; Trickett, Watts, & Birman, 1994). A common slogan displayed on buttons and t-shirts during Disability Awareness events on college campuses over the past several years claims "Attitudes are the real disability." According to Asch and Fine (1988), it is the attitudes of persons without disabilities that turn disabilities or limitations into "disabling" experiences. College climates and structures can marginalize students, creating barriers to their inclusion and success. Through such oppression emerge dichotomous structures of marginality and mattering (as defined by Schlossberg, 1989), inferiority and superiority, and disability and ability, resulting in an "us" and "them" culture. It is through the social construction of disability that colleges and universities can change their environments from oppression to inclusion. While attitudes toward disability are socially constructed, it is important to note that the physical, psychological, and other challenges faced by people with disabilities are very real. Pain is real. Needing to miss classes or needing a private room in the residence halls because of a physical condition are real needs that are not socially constructed.

The most recent paradigm of disability is the social justice perspective. This paradigm combines elements of the minority group model and the social construction framework. Referred to as the "disability oppression theory," Castaneda and Peters (2000) contend,

> *[It is] the pervasive and systematic nature of discrimination toward people with disabilities . . . [and] identifies the process to which people with disabilities journey toward power and liberation through the establishment of equitable access to accommodation within society's systems and through the creation of an interdependent social structure in which all persons are connected and depend on each other. (p. 320)*

The social justice paradigm focuses on the elimination of "ableism" as defined by Linton and Castaneda and Peters earlier in this chapter, and stresses "the dignity and right of every individual to a fulfilling educational experience" (Evans & Herriott, 2009).

Although most of these six frameworks (the moral model, the medical model, the functional limitations framework, the minority group paradigm, the social construction model, and the social justice perspective) allow professionals in higher education to provide services to students with disabilities, it is the social constructive model that leads professionals in all functional areas across the campus to focus beyond the disability and view the individual through a social lens, taking into account the person's interaction with his or her environment. In order to achieve this new perspective, Jones offers implications for practice using the SPAR model (Jacoby, 1993). She challenges all functional areas in higher education, which pride themselves on serving *all* students, to analyze each of the SPAR functions—services, programs, advocacy, and research—focusing specifically on students with disabilities and their lived experience. Disability itself is defined by environmental, structural, and cultural factors. By honing in on how students with disabilities interact with these factors when analyzing the quality of their SPAR functions, higher education professionals will gain a new perspective into the lives of their students and the socially constructed environment in which they live. Embracing the "shared experience" of ensuring the success of students with disabilities (Baxter Magolda, 1999; Bryan & Myers, 2006), faculty and staff together can remove the physical, social, and emotional barriers of the "disabling" environment, allowing all students to succeed. "[A] view of disability as socially constructed acknowledges that the experience of disability ultimately includes all persons" (Jones, 1996, p. 353). Research urges educators "to move beyond the limitation model of disability education and design curricula, programs, and services to be accessible to all people from the outset, no accommodations needed" (Myers, 2009a, p. 15).

Major Student Development Theories Related to Disability

Informed practitioners working in higher education understand that theory drives practice. As Evans (2008) stated, "knowing how to create an inclusive environment is a necessary but not sufficient condition for working effectively with students with disabilities. Educators must also understand the students themselves" (p. 11). In examining disability in the context of higher education, several major theories establish a basis for understanding disability identity development in students with disabilities, examining the college transition process for students with disabilities, and learning more about the importance of establishing meaningful relationships on campus for students with disabilities.

Studies by Troiano (2003) and Olkin (2003)

Focusing on the lived experiences of college students with disabilities has been instrumental in disability research. Troiano (2003) studied students with learning disabilities and focused on how the students make meaning of their college experience and their disability. To form an operational framework based on the students' lived experiences, Troiano discovered "the self-styled learning disability is comprised of four main properties: definition of the learning disability; orientation of the learning disability; condition of the learning disability; and impact of the learning disability" (p. 405). An additional study by Olkin (2003) addressed disability from a minority identity perspective, focusing on barriers faced by women with disabilities. Olkin (2003) posits that "being a woman and a person with a disability are not simply additive; rather, they interact synergistically" (p. 156). This interaction is frequently disadvantageous for women with disabilities, because they

TABLE 2
Disability Identity Development Model (Gibson, 2006)

Stage	One: Passive Awareness	Two: Realization	Three: Acceptance
Occurs	First part of life, can continue into adulthood	Occurs in adolescence/early adulthood	Adulthood
Interaction	No role model of disability; deny social aspects of disability	Begins to see self as having a disability; concerned with how others perceive self	Begins to see self as relevant; involves self in disability advocacy and activism
Characteristics	Codependency, shy away from attention	Self-hate, anger, concern with appearance	Shift focus from "being different" in a negative light to embracing self

experience greater detriments than they would as a result of their gender or disability status alone.

Disability Identity Development Model (Gibson, 2006)

Gibson (2006) developed a Disability Identity Development Model to help facilitate a better understanding of people with lifelong disabilities (i.e., early onset) by providing insight into possible struggles and perceptions experienced by a person with a disability. This three-stage approach can be helpful in working with people with disabilities, but Gibson warns against assuming that all people with disabilities fit into a particular stage. In addition, a person can move in and out of these three phases throughout their life, and just because a person reaches stage three does not mean they might not revert to stage one with a major life change or event. Table 2 illustrates each stage of the model.

Stage one of the Disability Identity Development Model (Gibson, 2006) is entitled "passive awareness." In this stage, a person with a disability is typically in the first part of their life; however, stage one can last into adulthood for certain people. The person has no role model of disability, and they are the most likely to deny any social aspects related to their disability. There is commonly a codependency in at least some aspect of their life, which can also be marked by a "good girl, good boy" relationship with others. A person with a disability has their medical needs met in this stage, but their disability becomes a silent member of their family. Most notably, the person shies away from attention in this stage.

In the second stage of this model, "realization," a person with a disability is usually in adolescence or early adulthood. This stage is a marked difference from the first "passive awareness" stage, because a person in stage two is truly beginning to see themselves as a person with a disability. This acknowledgment is frequently accompanied by self-hate, anger, and extreme concern over how others perceive them. Sometimes, a person in this stage will have a superman complex, or an unhealthy sense of personal responsibility. Finally, this stage is marked with a renewed concern about one's appearance (Gibson, 2006).

In the third and final stage of the model, entitled "acceptance," a person with a disability no longer sees "being different" as a negative, and has begun to fully embrace themselves. In addition, the person sees themselves as relevant and no less than a person without a disability. This third stage includes a social aspect, where the individual with a disability begins to socialize with other people with disabilities and sometimes even gets involved in disability advocacy and activism efforts. Most profoundly, people with disabilities in this phase have begun to integrate themselves fully into the world, rather than keeping a physical or psychological distance in some aspects of their lives (Gibson, 2006).

Onset of disability often determines whether or not the student is willing or ready to disclose the disability, and onset also might determine the type of accommodation requested or needed. Despite when a student acquired a disability, a student in the realization or acceptance stage of Gibson's Disability Identity Development Model (Gibson, 2011) may be comfortable requesting large print for handouts and extended time for exams, whereas a student in the passive-awareness stage of Gibson's model might not see a need or have the confidence to request accommodations. Students with early onset of disabilities most likely have experienced accommodations throughout their lifetimes and are knowledgeable of the types of accommodations needed. A student with recent hearing loss may need real-time captioning rather than a sign language interpreter. Students who acquired disabilities later in life such as students with spinal cord injuries or traumatic brain injuries, who lost limbs from accidents, or who have post-traumatic stress disorder (PTSD) might be unsure as to what they need to succeed in college and unskilled in asking for such accommodations.

In addition, the accommodations themselves may be different for students with early onset of disability than those required by students with later onset. For example, students with early onset of hearing loss might need real-time captioning whereas students who were born deaf may need sign language interpreters. Even when universal design is widely adopted, there are still specific accommodations that may need to be provided such as Braille for students who are blind. It is important to note, however, only 10% of people who are blind use Braille (National Federation for the Blind, 2013). The majority of students who are blind use audio books and screen reader software. Awareness of the difference in readiness and development of students with disabilities and their disability onset is imperative for higher education professionals when advising, counseling, and accommodating students.

The Transition Theory (Schlossberg, Waters, & Goodman, 1995)
Another theory that is helpful when working with students with disabilities is The Transition Theory (Schlossberg et al., 1995). Transition, as outlined by this theory is "any event, or nonevent, that results in changed relationships, routines, assumptions, and roles" (Schlossberg et al., 1995, p. 27). In order for a person to fully grasp what a transition means to an individual, there must be an understanding of the nature, background, and impact of the transition. In order to cope with a transition effectively, the Transition Theory identifies four major factors (the "four S's"), which are situation, self, support, and strategies. To ponder one's "situation" includes a consideration of issues such as timing, duration, control, concurrent stress, and role change. An analysis of "self" includes looking at personal and demographic characteristics like age, stage of life, and one's gender. "Support" is looked at in terms of type of support, function of the support, and ways to measure that support, while

"strategy," the fourth "S," analyzes methods of copying employed by the individual. This theory also discusses the impact of a nonevent, which is described as an expected transition that does not in fact occur.

The Theory of Marginality and Mattering (Schlossberg, 1989)

The Theory of Marginality and Mattering (Schlossberg, 1989) is another theory relevant to disability in higher education. Schlossberg discusses the importance of mattering and the impact of marginality in the college experience and a student's development. Marginalization occurs when students enter new roles, especially when the new roles are uncertain or ambiguous. These feelings can lead students to feel like they do not fit in with others, which can then lead to more serious feelings of insecurity, depression, and extreme self-consciousness. Schlossberg emphasizes the imperative role that colleges and universities have in helping students feel like they matter to others.

Attitudes Toward Disability

Disability can be a visible or hidden identity. The multiple identities within the disability community—physical, cognitive, and psychological—create a vast spectrum of individualized experiences for individuals with a disability. Such complexity often means that individuals within the disability community experience societal barriers and attitudes quite differently. In addition to each person's unique lived experiences, there is a transcendental emergence of the harmful effects from ableism, microaggressions, stereotypes, misconceptions, and generalizations.

The attitudinal approach toward people with disabilities has a large influence on creating a positive campus climate. Individuals with disabilities experience inclusion on a campus through the attitudes of peers, faculty, staff, and administrators. Access for students through accommodations and modifications are measures of inclusion; attitudes that create welcoming environments are critical, significant contributors to inclusion as well (Kalivoda, 2009). Attitudes are rooted in the historical context of identity and the social constructs through which the identity has evolved. Disability has been a stigmatized identity in the United States largely due to the early moral and medical models that shaped the societal perception of what traditionally is considered ability. Ableism, the systemic discrimination of people with disabilities (Castaneda & Peters, 2000), has allowed for negative attitudes toward disability to prevail.

For people with disabilities, the accepted use of separate accommodations often results in a damaging experience. A pervasive notion across all levels of education is that separate is accommodating and helpful to people with disabilities. However, from the labels of "special education," "special considerations," or "special needs," the word "special" has taken on a negative connotation and carries an implication that individuals forced into these brandings are exceptions rather than people to be included. The combination of separate accommodations and the "special" label can influence the attitudinal approach of children who otherwise would not have been viewed people with disabilities as exclusions. McCarthy (2011) states, "the implication of special considerations is that there is some reason a student cannot meet regular requirements; the student is less than the norm" (p. 299). Separate does not mean equal. This truth can be viewed in the attitudes created through the idea of separation, rather than inclusion, which ironically ends in inequality of treatment.

Conner and Baglieri (2009) state, "It can be argued that it is the attitudes toward those deemed abnormal that actively causes their disablement, not their physical or sensory impairment or their perceived lack of cognitive ability or 'appropriate' behaviors" (p. 342). Attitudes and labels place the stigma of disability on individuals. Labeling is related to the social construction of identity, and labels have often been cultivated by those with privilege as a way to collectively marginalize and oppress certain identities. The groups that are targeted are often deemed as deviant from the norm and incur negative labels and attitudes.

Many people do not recognize the historical context of the labels society has created. Several targeted groups may attempt to take ownership and try to empower themselves as part of a community; however, the initial labeling and grouping is due to the lack of adherence to a societal "normative." Labels attempt to simplify a person through a defined word or phrase. This practice is inherently harmful as people are multidimensional and carry more than just the selected identity label. More importantly, mislabeling or identifying someone can cause great psychological harm to a person by altering one's sense of self-concept and self-worth in society. Labels can be difficult to fight and even harder to overcome. Labeling people with whom they do not identify changes their sense of self-efficacy both to them and to others in society.

Attitudes toward people with disabilities are challenged greatly by the complexity of intersections of identity. Individuals with multiple marginalized identities not only will battle the stigma associated with having a disability but also may have to combat additional negative attitudes toward their disability from other identity communities. Similarly, they may have to endure the consequences of negative attitudes toward their other marginalized, salient identities from the disability community. To assist with the illustration of how intersections of identity can be difficult to navigate due to societal expectations and attitudes, consider the following: A man with a physical disability often will be stereotypically viewed as not dominant, dependent on others, emotional, and/or not competitive (Gordon & Rosenblum, 2001). This contrasts with the expectation that men in society must be tough, strong, competitive, independent, and unemotional (Edwards & Jones, 2009). The direct conflict between how a person with a disability is perceived in society and the expectations of men in society frequently leads to emasculating men with disabilities. This simplistic reduction has significant consequences for men with disabilities, particularly in the areas of self-worth and relationships with others.

Society's attitudes are brought into the institution from each individual who attends. It is important to focus intentionally on campus environments that create inclusive campus climates for students (Harper, 2008). Attitudes toward people with disabilities on campus usually reflect a variety of perspectives from inclusion and acceptance to discrimination and prejudice. These attitudes can be systemic or individual. Although faculty, staff, and administrators are compelled by law to make reasonable accommodations for students, climate goes far beyond doing the minimum required; attitudes must be balanced. Unfortunately, covert attitudes are some of the most difficult to address since individuals often do not understand the challenges brought about by their perspectives.

Questions of what is fair for students with disabilities arise in the context of the classroom setting frequently. McCarthy (2011) speaks to the idea of "fairness" which is an attitudinal approach of privilege often taken from the moral model. Is it fair to give a student with a disability more time to complete an assignment? Is it fair to other students to take classroom time to provide instruction to a student with a disability? Is it fair to grade a student with a disability on a different grading system than the other students? These questions of fairness shed light on a system of equals. The binary system of equality (fair or not fair) does not appropriately reflect the needs of individuals. Rather, this approach leads to confused and sometimes harsh attitudes toward the people with disabilities. Society must embrace equity rather than equality. The idea of what is equitable for a student brings an individual approach to the education of students with disabilities. The individual understanding of various student needs can also lead to a shift in attitudinal approach, away from what is fair and toward what is valuable.

Microaggressions are another example of overt or covert harmful attitudes toward marginalized individuals. Microaggressions are described as common and subtle verbal, visual, or behavioral actions that communicate negative, derogatory, or inimical insults that psychologically impact marginalized individuals or groups (Solorzano, Ceja, & Yosso, 2000). Sue and Capodilupo (2008) illustrate the negative impact of racial, gender, and sexual orientation microaggressions on marginalized groups and individuals and the concept can easily be translated to the experiences of people with disabilities. A common example of microaggressing people with disabilities is to assume an individual with a physical disability needs someone else to do a task for them, thus implying that the person is helpless. Another example of microaggression is when people without disabilities act surprised after a person with a disability speaks about a significant other: This surprise sends the message that people with disabilities are desexualized. These invalidations or direct insults can cause significant immediate distress to recipients and may create, over time, negative self-images for people with disabilities.

The cyclical nature of systems and attitudes toward individuals with disabilities appears almost inseparable. Yet, one must be strong enough in conviction to interrupt the dogma that reinforces disability as an abnormality. For true change, one must begin to challenge the social processes through which disability is viewed (i.e., moral model, medical model, and functional limitations model). If overall societal views toward disability shift, it becomes easier to confront the attitudes of individuals, as the systems will no longer support those perspectives.

Disability Services on Campus

A disability support service office has a responsibility to provide access to all aspects of the institution for students with disabilities. Often this access and support comes in the form of accommodations. However, disability support services can also be responsible for legal compliance, documentation of students with disabilities, university policies regarding disability support, and training for faculty and staff on working with students with disabilities. Disability services are designed differently based on the institutional need and institutional structures, but the primary mission is access.

According to the Council for the Advancement of Standards (CAS) in Higher Education (2012), the demands of disability services require a strong comprehension of medical conditions, curricular and cocurricular needs and demands, assessment of various types of abilities, technological advances such as screen readers and speech output, campus safety, and distance education, among some of the namable responsibilities. Some of the typical accommodations McCarthy (2011) cites are "additional time on exams, copies of notes from classmates, reduced-distraction testing environments" (p. 300). The challenge is promoting student learning and development while managing responsibilities and duties to the students, particularly with the overlay of legal compliance requirements.

McCarthy (2007) highlights the idea of self-advocacy as a necessity in American higher education for students with disabilities. Additionally, there is a need for student learning prompted by reflection, asking questions, and encouraging independent decision making in order to assist students with disabilities develop a stronger sense of self-reliance and self-efficacy (Bandura, 1977). Advising a student with a disability can extend the ideas of mattering and marginality (Schlossberg, 1989) as well as help the student build a strong sense of self-efficacy.

One of the challenges disability support services must tackle is how to balance the need to serve as a clearinghouse to ensure students are being provided access and accommodations, while encouraging the rest of the campus community to take ownership for inclusion of students with disabilities. Every faculty, staff, and administrator has a responsibility to assess current curriculum, initiatives, events, and services for access for people with disabilities. Disability support services can consult with various departments and individuals on campus to assist with knowledge acquisition related to disability. Additionally, introducing a competencies model for goal achievement to demonstrate learning can occur through multiple modalities (Evans et al., 2009), which will accommodate a variety of learners. Open communication with learners is required to understand students' strengths, weaknesses, and goals (Haverkos, 2011).

One of the recommended shifts in higher education is to work with students individually to structure academic plans for each learner (Haverkos, 2011). Currently, the blanket approach of working with students to provide standard accommodations does not meet the individual need of each student. Additionally, this approach can lead to unnecessary accommodations being made that do not appropriately challenge a student. A team approach including faculty, staff, academic advisors, student health and counseling, and disability support services to develop an individual, holistically focused plan for each student would be ideal. This model reinserts some of the history of faculty involvement with students throughout their education (Rudolph, 1990).

By law (ADA, 1990), equal access through reasonable accommodation must be provided for students with disabilities. Equal access, however, poses a challenge for college students in that it does not provide tailored access for individual students. It also results in a dichotomous system of students with disabilities and students without disabilities. Taking an approach to assist the campus community in creating inclusive environments would require equitable access for students with disabilities rather than simply equal access for these students.

Student Veterans With Disabilities

Since the 1950s, veterans with disabilities have sparked colleges and universities to re-think student services and develop programs that aid with all processes of earning a postsecondary degree. According to the American Council on Education (ACE, 2008), an estimated two million veterans of the Iraq and Afghanistan wars will return to the United States and enroll in college. Many of these student veterans will have a range of disabilities that could impact their college experience (Madaus, Miller, & Vance, 2009), including an estimated 20% of veterans experiencing post-traumatic stress disorder or major depression, and an estimated 19% of veterans experiencing a traumatic brain injury (RAND Center for Military Health Policy Research, 2008). These disabilities, along with potential learning disabilities or attention deficit/hyperactivity disorder (ADHD), are considered "hidden" disabilities and may not be noticeable upon first interactions with the student. Other veterans will have physical disabilities as a result of their time spent in combat. For many student veterans with disabilities, the challenge of postsecondary education is significant (Madaus et al., 2009).

Currently, the Americans with Disabilities Act and Section 504 of the Rehabilitation Act of 1973 establish the requirement that colleges and universities accommodate students with disabilities. However, it is the student's responsibility to disclose his or her disability and seek accommodations upon entering college. For student veterans with disabilities, this process presents several challenges. First, many student veterans have invisible disabilities resulting from the time they served in a war. "Student veterans, as well as veterans generally, are often hesitant to self-identify these and other disabilities acquired during their military service" (Shackelford, 2009, p. 36). In addition, student veterans might have psychological or learning disabilities that were undiagnosed prior to enlisting in the military. As years transpired during their military service, these learning disabilities might have intensified, and as the student veteran enters college, the disability is more noticeable; however, the disability is undocumented. In addition, it is not uncommon for evaluations, diagnoses, and documentation of a student veteran's disability to require a Disability Services office on campus to interact with certain governmental bureaucracy, which can be time consuming and tedious (Shackelford, 2009).

As Grossman (2009) notes,

> *these challenges present a great opportunity for reinvigoration of the disability rights movement by the veterans, and others, as well as innovation, the development of best practices, and the adoption of Universal Design (UD) solutions by colleges and universities committed to effectively addressing the civil rights of this new population of students with disabilities. (p. 4)*

Students with disabilities on college campuses are not solely the responsibility of Disability Services offices. It is up to all faculty, staff, and administrators at postsecondary institutions to be accommodating and find ways to make programs, classes, and physical spaces accessible for all students. Disability Services offices at institutions across the country, however, must be prepared to process paperwork and handle all other necessary components of the accommodation process for student veterans with disabilities. As Madaus et al. (2009) point out, "as always, the requirement to be sensitive to the situation of the student being advised is paramount, and it should be understood that combat veterans with disabilities have challenges only those who have served in combat can understand" (p. 14). In addition, the different perspective of a veteran might cause a different approach to the disability disclosure and accommodation-seeking service process (Burnett & Segoria, 2009).

Conclusion

A discussion of campus complexity and disability tends to begin with the major models of disability, student development theories related to disability, and attitudes toward disability. Such models and theories have been and continue to be used as the foundational structure for disability services provided at colleges and universities. Attention to various populations of students with disabilities including returning military students, nontraditional students, international students, and students with temporary disabilities is essential in developing a respectful, welcoming, inclusive campus climate.

Increasing Awareness: Allies, Advocacy, and the Campus Community

> Our capacity to generate excitement is deeply affected by our interest in one another, in hearing one another's voices, in recognizing one another's presence.
>
> bell hooks (1994, p. 8)

IN ORDER TO ACTUALIZE BEING AN ally for people with disabilities and the disability community, it is vital to begin with an understanding of what it means to be an ally for identity-based groups. It can take one years to dissect, understand, and most importantly develop awareness around this concept of allyhood. Due to the distinct process of ally development that involves an individual's ability to cognitively grow and personally reflect, it is impossible to write a chapter or a book that describes step-by-step what a person must do to become an ally. The following pages could be filled with dos and don'ts of allyhood and yet, reading and comprehending all of those pages would still not make one an ally. Being an ally is about attitude, awareness, and behavior. There is no easy process to becoming an ally and there are no checkboxes that will certify someone an ally. However, through knowledge acquisition, immersion in a community, and lots of trial and error, one may eventually be granted the title of ally. In the following chapter, the concepts of allyhood and advocacy, associated theoretical frameworks, group memberships involved in ally identities, praxis, and pragmatic recommendations for being an ally for people with disabilities are explored and discussed.

Defining Ally

The process and positionality of allyhood can be very personal. Being an ally is an intentional choice that impacts one's behavior, thought, and action. One cannot become an ally without full consciousness of one's responsibility to the community of which you are an ally. While over time some ally-related actions may seem less deliberate, as the identity becomes integrated, the level of self-awareness and consciousness must remain present.

An ally can be defined as an agent group member working for social change rather than for oppression (Wijeyesinghe, Griffin, & Love, 1997); members of dominant social groups, with greater privilege, working to end the system of oppression (Broido, 2000); and individuals within marginalized groups supporting subdominant groups (Casey-Powell & Souma, 2009). For the purposes of this chapter, a broad definition of the term ally is utilized: individuals working to end the victimization, marginalization, and oppression of social subordinated groups. Additionally, given the focus on ally development for the disability community, allies are not necessarily part of the dominant or privileged culture. While most allies tend to be those with privileged identities, and allies from the majority are necessary for change, the discussion of allies within a community is fundamental as well. This is a particularly salient point when speaking about allies for people with disabilities, as the disability community is so varied in sub-identity. The community encompasses a range of physical, psychological, and cognitive abilities. Due to the varying physical and social barriers for each identity, it is important to distinguish awareness that one particular identity does not automatically equate to "allyhood" for all identities under the disability umbrella term.

Social justice is often utilized in Higher Education as a catchall phrase—one that implies the representation of diverse communities, accepts people from underrepresented social identities, and appreciates or tolerates multiculturalism in the population at the institution. Social justice, in this sense, is an oversimplified buzzword conflated with diversity and multiculturalism. As an ally, one needs to understand the term social justice and how the concepts of true social justice are necessary for allyhood. Social justice addresses the concepts of power, privilege, and oppression. Each of these concepts, individually examined, provides a different context for which one should actively consider in practice an ally.

People from dominant groups engage as allies for various motives including empathy, moral principles, spiritual values, and self-interest (Goodman, 2001). As an ally, it is important to understand one's motives for being invested in the work. No one motive will resonate for all allies. Identifying motive is beneficial for the individual ally's development, and for those facilitating ally development or educational efforts. Being an ally is not about "being one of the good ones" rather, it is about acting for positive social change, which can occur for marginalized groups as a result of ally participation.

As an ally, one will need to understand and embrace the concept of vulnerability. As an ally to the disability community, one must accept each individual marginalized group member's experiences, responses, wishes, and needs. Each member requires a different and unique response from allies. Additionally, allies can often feel uncomfortable with the idea of not knowing the needs of a specific community, not having complete knowledge of or not knowing what obstacles or opinions lie ahead. An ally must be comfortable with being vulnerable to the questions, being vulnerable to and in front of other people, and being vulnerable to the unknown journey. Allyhood is a dynamic, multilayered, constantly shifting, and changing process. These characteristics are necessary to embrace as they align with the dynamic and changing nature of social construction.

Allyhood does not require one to hold a complete and total knowledge about a community. However, being an ally does require one to have an investment in the lifelong learning of a particular or multiple communities. Allies must shift away from the expectation that people identifying with a minority identity must hold expert knowledge about their own community. This is simply not the case. Each person with a minority identity has a powerful personal narrative to contribute. At the same time, there is learning to be had about group identity, power, privilege, and oppression. Thus, shifting the expectation that allies will become experts on identity before truly being advocates or involved in the narrative is vital. A lack of consciousness or awareness from a majority-identified person does not equate to a lack of involvement in the system. All persons are participants in the system already, either supporting hegemony or working against it. Both dominants and subordinates are already involved by the very composition of the existing social systems. So, learning as one goes provides a more realistic expectation of knowledge acquisition. Everyone will continue learning, evolving, and making mistakes along the way.

Advocates for disability and social justice argue disability is created by society through "imposing standards of normalcy that exclude those who are different physically, emotionally, or cognitively" (Evans, Assadi, & Herriott, 2005, p. 67). One must conceptualize the importance of allies of people with disabilities, advocacy, and activism on college campuses (Evans & Herriott, 2009; Higbee & Mitchell, 2009). Within the context of higher education, an ally can be viewed as someone changing the campus, which includes advocating to improve representation, policies, available resources, and education around inclusion. An ally can also be viewed as a person working with individuals to assist their identity development or navigation of the institutional environment. Regardless of choosing to be an ally for individuals or larger systemic change, being an ally means more than a plaque on a door or a verbal promise. Being an ally is the *attitudinal position* of a person, the *willingness to learn* about an identity, and the *actions taken* as a mark of commitment.

Membership

The power of systems of oppression and privilege are propelled by individual actions and behaviors. Each person has a responsibility to examine their own positionality within the system, understand where one colludes with the system, and where one can evoke change. An examination of group membership is critical to recognize for ally development. Knowledge of where one is oppressed and where one is privileged assists with progressing through the development stages. This is not to say that by the very nature of being in a subordinate group, one has automatic knowledge of the systems for that group. However, lived experience will contribute to the lens through which one understands power, privilege, and oppression of the disability community. For many, identifying with a dominant or subordinate group may be easily reconciled or communicated. People do not fit neatly into the social constructs of identity that society has created. Identity is complex and nondichotomous; membership as allies must be explored for majority and minority identities. This is with the recognition that people have multiple dimensions of identity (Abes, Jones, & McEwen, 2007; Jones & McEwen, 2000) and will not identify stagnantly with one group at all times. Given the evolving and fluid nature of identity dimensions, a person's positionality and saliency of identity dimensions can shift. As meaning-making capacity interacts with context, social identity salience, and core identity valued characteristics, one begins to understand individual identity and how relationships are perceived based on identity. Allies therefore can develop a deeper sense of self-identity and a deeper appreciation for the salient identity dimensions of others.

Allies From Majority Identities

Members of majority identities must challenge themselves as allies to interrogate every corner of socialization. How has one come to understand the society in which one lives? How often does one think about one's identities? How does one experience daily life in society? Answering these questions requires a look into the ideas around internalized and socialized notions of self and concepts around privilege. Bell (1997) stated, "Internalized domination is the incorporation and acceptance by individuals within the dominant group of prejudices against others and the assumption that the status quo is normal and correct" (p. 12). There is a lack of consciousness that occurs for most people with majority identities. Until one begins to consciously explore positionality, one cannot begin the journey to allyhood.

Regardless of the particular social construction or social issue working with members of majority identities, also considered privileged, dominant, and agent identities, is similar (Goodman, 2001). Each axis of oppression and minority group has its own characteristics, cultural nuances, and group dynamics to appreciate. As such, being an ally for one community does not mean being an ally to all communities. Furthermore, one can be invested in the idea of eradicating social injustice and inequality, but that does not make a person an ally. An ally requires action. And without the proper knowledge of self and the particular communities encompassed by oppression, utilizing the blanket term ally to encompass a majority person's interactions with all marginalized communities does not seem appropriate. There is a distinction of identity in each minority community, requiring those in a majority identity to cyclically move through the developmental process of being an ally for and with each community. As an ally, one must understand the individual experience from identity to identity.

Additionally, members of majority identities often self-select the title ally to show support or solidarity with a community. Ally is not a title to be selected but rather bestowed upon an individual. If a member of the majority is operating from purely altruistic motives, the title becomes insignificant, as the work toward social change is paramount. It is important to not conflate the desire for the title of ally with someone seeking approval from a minority group. As an ally, one must have a strong sense of self-efficacy (Bandura, 1977) so as to not be seeking constant approval or praise from the marginalized group.

Allies Within Community

Allies are not just an identity for those with a privileged social identity. Allies also include individuals within marginalized communities. One may hold a particular oppressed social identity, but the self-identification with an identity does not equate to automatic allyhood for the same community. Bell (1997) stated, "Internalized acceptance of the status quo among subordinate groups can also lead them to turn on members of the group who challenge it. This horizontal hostility blocks solidarity among group members and prevents organizing for change" (p. 12). The causes of horizontal hostility can be viewed through the framework of identity development theory. Many psychosocial theories demonstrate the lack of development could lead to horizontal blocking. For several minority identity development theorists such as Cass (1979), Cross (1995), Phinney (1989), and Gibson (2006), one must move from denial of identity and identification with societal indoctrination to acceptance, embracing, understanding, and empowering one's identity. Until an individual has progressed in one's own identity development, they may collude with oppressive acts or ideas.

Minority groups are clustered together under umbrella terms such as the disability community, people of color community, lesbian, gay, bisexual and transgender community, religious minority community, and the gender non-conforming community. There is a vast array of gradations within each of these communities that requires even members of the minority group to be educated about so as not to oppress one another. For example, in the disability community, there is a large range of physical, cognitive, and psychological disabilities. The needs of one individual who is deaf will contrast significantly from an individual with a learning disability. Allies must form within minority communities due to the nature of composite of identity into large lumped categories. Every person can become an ally for a group, cause, or identity in order to end the isms.

Theories of Ally Development

The theoretical frameworks presented provide a lens for which to view the development of allies. Each of these models presents a different viewpoint on the journey to become an ally. While the factors, statuses, and steps vary between models, the comprehensive picture speaks volumes for the multifaceted development of ally personal discovery and knowledge acquisition. Collectively the models expose the emotional and intellectual process of becoming an ally.

Broido's Model of College Student Ally Development
The Broido Model of Social Justice Ally Development (Broido, 2000) is based on a study of the development of six (three male and three female), White,

heterosexual students attitudes toward developing their ally identity. The most significant influences and outcomes are summarized by several factors.

The participants in the study displayed *pre-college egalitarian values* that align with the purposes of social justice work. These values must be taken into account when looking at the generalizability of the study. The participants previously believed discrimination was unjust and people should be fundamentally equal.

The *acquisition of information* was considered critical to participants. *Content* was deemed important as the participants engaged with varying information related to the experiences of target and dominant group members, the benefits of diversity, the facts and existence of oppression, and how oppression impacts target group members. Additionally, *information sources* were critical as the participants reflected from where they derived information. Largely, the classroom was cited as a source of information, specifically courses which discuss issues of social justice in supportive environments. Several participants also cited independent reading as an important source of knowledge. The final major source of information was directly from target group members in a variety of educational conversation settings. These conversations were important for gaining facts and additional perspectives on social justice.

Participants spoke to the importance of employing *meaning-making* strategies such as concurrently acquiring information, discussing the information, and reflecting on the information. Participants gave examples of active *discussion* occurring as an important component of developing ally perspectives. Discussion largely took place again in classrooms and among peers in nonstructure formats. *Perspective-taking* assisted participants in varying their viewpoints from engaging with others. Participants also attempted to take on the perspective of target group members. Subsequently, participants developed their own positions on issues. *Self-reflection* encompassed part of the process between perspective taking and developing a position. Participants had to take the time to understand their own values and positions. These *multiple methods of meaning making* often happened simultaneously and without distinction between strategies. The process of meaning making was central to the development of participants.

Self-confidence was critical to the progress of participants' ally development. Worth, approval, self-esteem, self-worth, physical safety, and identities were threatened at varying levels during the meaning making and development process for participants. Building self-confidence, through experiences in college and developing less dependency on peers, allowed participants to dissect their privilege but also move forward as allies.

Finally, *recruitment* into action and the process of becoming an ally was a primary factor. Some participants held positions where ally behavior was expected and prompted their call to action. The actions were not initially self-initiated but became a commitment for participants.

Edwards Aspiring Social Justice Ally Development Model

The Edwards Model for Aspiring Social Justice Ally Identity Development (Edwards, 2006) presents three, nonlinear, developmental statuses of aspiring ally identities. The goal of development is to promote complex, sustainable consciousness. This model provides aspiring allies a frame to better understand their own experiences, a marker for accountability, and an aspirational goal for development.

An *Ally for Self-Interest* is motivated to protect those one knows and cares about. This person may not identify with the term ally. One's involvement or intervention is on behalf of an individual to whom one is connected rather than to a larger community or group issue. An Ally for Self-Interest is unable to connect individual acts of oppression to the larger system. This person is unlikely to confront acts of oppression if the individual to whom one is connected is not present. An Ally for Self-Interest believes one is acting from a place of care, doing the "right thing," but may perpetuate oppressive behavior due to unacknowledged privilege.

In the university environment, this status is frequently observed between students. For example, an undergraduate student has a sibling with autism. The student has advocated for the sibling, ensured the sibling had positive interactions with others, and challenged harmful comments made by others. But the student is unable to connect these actions to his or her own behavior outside of the sibling. The student might in turn participate in the alienation of a peer on a residence hall floor with social interaction difficulties due to

Asperger's, rather than considering the broad spectrum of autism. The student may do this somewhat unintentionally because the student never considered the sibling as one of many with autism. The lack of examining the identity or system has left the student unable to challenge discrimination beyond isolated instances with the sibling present.

The *Aspiring Ally for Altruism* often experiences the underlying emotion of guilt as one comes to comprehend systems of oppression. As a result, an Aspiring Ally for Altruism will vilify other members of dominant groups. This is done in order to distance oneself from the responsibility of oppression as a member of a dominant group and continue to be seen as "one of the good ones." It can be difficult for the Aspiring Ally for Altruism to speak with and not for oppressed groups; this almost paternalistic approach leads one to maintain control rather than support oppressed groups to be in control. Ultimately an Aspiring Ally for Altruism sees one's efforts as selfless and should be welcomed by oppressed groups.

For example, a staff member at a university working with a student with a physical disability may start serving as a resource for the student. The student needs assistance with making the campus more accessible so the student can easily move between buildings for class. The staff member may begin to confront individual faculty, staff, and students on not assisting the student with the physical disability. By confronting individuals, the staff member identifies the role of advocate through an individual change lens. However, this is a reactive response and does not work toward the systemic accessibility issues the student is experiencing. The staff member might become more immersed in championing issues of physical disability as a voice for the community rather than taking opportunities to include the student in the conversation.

An *Ally for Social Justice* works with those from oppressed groups building a coalition to end systems of oppression. This person is collaborative, recognizing ending systems benefits target and agent groups. This person works with agent groups to take responsibility for their role in the system rather than separate oneself from those groups. An Ally for Social Justice demonstrates sustained passion for social justice. This person often seeks critique, accepts responsibility, and does not hinge one's investment on praise from oppressed groups.

For example, a professor notices a student with a learning disability is struggling with class assignments. The professor begins to engage in a conversation with the student about what methods of learning are most effective for the student. Through this conversation the professor learns the resources on campus are limited for students with learning disabilities, and, in order to properly support students, need to become much more expansive. The professor begins to invite the student into various university stakeholder meetings to advocate for more resources. The professor also raises issues of resources, determination of course assignments, and varied learning methods at department meetings. A student confronts the professor in the next semester about an assignment that is not conducive to particular learning styles. The professor takes the feedback and uses it to change the assignment for the following semester. The professor is demonstrating how to empower a community to have a voice, creating access without being in the spotlight, and advocating for systemic change from within through university services and department meetings with colleagues.

Bishop's Six-Step Model to Becoming an Ally

Bishop (2002) stated knowledge of the process of how and why people chose to give up privilege is crucial insight to social change; knowledge of the process assisting in overcoming all types of oppression. Bishop provides a narrative of unlearning racism and heterosexism. Additionally, she speaks to the problematic competition among oppressed groups, reinforcing each other's oppression by creating a hierarchy, instead of combining energy to fight the source of all oppression.

Bishop outlines six steps involved in becoming an ally from her own experience. The first step is *understanding oppression*, how it evolved, how it has remained, and the patterns consistently reestablished by individuals and institutional systems. Second, one can *understand different oppressions,* how they compare, and how they strengthen one another, and the interactions of these oppressions. Third, one can develop in *consciousness and healing.* Pain accompanies the increased understanding in one's role in the cycle of oppression. In order to break the cycle and grow as an ally, one must break the silences and begin healing the pain. Fourth, one must *work on one's own liberation* from areas of oppression. This requires reflection on how oppression has impacted one's own life and how to take action for change. The fifth step *becoming an ally* requires one to examine previous roles as an oppressor. Each person is required to learn new skills, such as listening, supporting oppressed groups, and educating dominant groups. An individual is then moving toward a new emancipation from the system of oppression. Finally, the sixth step is *maintaining hope*. Working toward social change is a long journey that can be liberating and painful. It is important to keep in mind the goal is to develop social, political, and economic structures that benefit everyone.

Washington and Evans's Model for Becoming an Ally

Washington and Evans present a model of four developmental levels of becoming an ally (Washington & Evans, 1991). First, *awareness* is the exploration of differences and similarities of self to the oppressed group. Understanding stereotypes, stigmas, and assumptions is essential to raising one's own awareness. Self-examination of one's own identity is also important. Next is *education,* rooted in knowledge acquisition of policies, laws, practices, movements, language, and symbols. Knowledge can be developed through a variety of modalities such as interaction with oppressed persons, exploration through literature, art, and workshops. Third is developing the *skills*, which can be refined through workshops, dialogues, mentoring, and engaging with the community. After the three developmental levels, one is called to *action*. One is asked then to effect change in the lives of others, social structure, and institutional systems informed by the development of the first three levels.

Praxis

As an ally, it is important to recognize the Freireian idea that action and reflection are required for true word. And "true word is equal to the work, which is equal to praxis" (Freire, 2004, p. 87). Praxis for ally development reflects the idea of infusing knowledge acquisition with practical application in order to evoke change. As Freire implies, neither component has primacy; each is equally important to transformation.

Each individual, as an ally, needs to determine their investment in the social landscape. One must determine what they are going to be an ally for and to what level they are dedicated to that particular social issue. The dedication and subject of social issues can change over time as the landscape shifts and as allies further develop a broader understanding of oppression. Ally education can and should be viewed through a learning paradigm. Allies, like learners, must be active participants, consumers of knowledge, in their own self-actualization (hooks, 1994).

The practice of being an ally requires one to be intentional in both thought and action. The idea of being an ally is driven from more than existence in a space alone; one cannot keep silent. Each individual committing to the identity of being an ally must in fact be an active participant in the identity. Ally requires action, advocacy, and practice. Unlike other social identities, one must be engaged in the work of an ally in order to maintain the identity as the definition of an ally is rooted in action. One cannot be an ally for a community while colluding with societal norms and standards, sitting silently at times of injustice—this is the antithesis of an ally, which requires action.

Henry Giroux (2005) spoke of the idea of border pedagogy: not just recognizing differences, culture, history, and social margins, but also challenging the existing boundaries, creating space to insert differences, and contradictory voices, expanding the borders inherited and previously framed. Giroux encourages border crossing for educators:

> *Critical educators cannot be content just to merely map how ideologies are inscribed in the various relations of schooling, whether they be the curriculum, forms of school organization, or in teacher-student relations . . . a more viable critical pedagogy need to go beyond them analyzing how ideologies are actually taken-up in the voices and lived experiences of students ... provide the conditions for students to speak so that their narratives can be affirmed and engaged along with the consistencies and contradictions that characterize such experiences. (p. 145)*

Giroux highlights the importance of individual actions, active measures taken, in order to change the pedagogical landscape as an ally for decreasing the pervasive dominant narrative. Being an ally is both being active and being an advocate.

Community of Allies

Motives for one to become an ally are often discussed in social justice conversations, but not as frequently if there is a focus on the difficulty of being an ally. One can experience isolation as an ally. For some allies, acceptance into a marginalized community can occur; however, this is dependent on the particular relationships among individuals. An ally will never fully understand the scope of being a member of the marginalized community. Despite all of the awareness, knowledge, thought, action, and advocacy, a member of a privileged identity still does not have the lived experience of a marginalized member of society. The work of an ally can be difficult with perseverance diminishing over time. In the field of higher education and providing a positive campus environment, Boyer (1990) proposed six characteristics for a community of learning: purposefulness, openness, justice, discipline, caring, and celebratory. Utilizing the same characteristics, an ally community can be formed in order to provide an environment for continued learning and support, thus creating a support system with other allies can reduce isolation and burnout.

Allies for Disability: A Paradigm for Support

Discovering one's capacity as an ally for disability can be viewed on the individual level, group level, or the systemic level (Hardiman & Jackson, 1997). On the individual level, a person beginning to develop awareness, and enter into information gathering may have key questions regarding interaction with individuals with disabilities such as, "What should I do?"; "How should I respond?"; and "Is it okay to say that?" The short answer is one should ask individuals one is interacting with as it varies from person to person. Asking questions allows one to understand individual preference as well as better understand the person with a disability's viewpoint. As an example, one can ask a person with a visual impairment if they need assistance rather than just doing a task for the person. Additionally, on the individual level, an ally can become more cognizant of the language being utilized when referring to individuals in the disability community (Rauscher & McClintock, 1997). Examples of person-first language and specific sub-identities of the disability umbrella are provided in the first chapter.

Creating an institutional climate of inclusion for disability requires a shift not only in paradigm for viewing disability but also in administrative notions of institutional resources. Disability support is mostly viewed in higher education through a functional limitations model (Hahn, 1988), where the individual is accommodated as needed and typically in separate but not equal ways. Focusing only on the individual's needs in a reactive manner does not address the environmental larger system issue of inclusion, therefore implying the environment does not need to change but the individual does (Jones, 1996). This continues to perpetuate oppression of people with disabilities. As Jones suggests, moving to a social construction framework "acknowledges the power of environmental, structural, and cultural definitions of disability" (p. 353). The change to a social construction model can drastically improve the campus climate for individuals with a disability.

Continuing to examine the ways in which higher education employs the functional limitations model is part of ally development. Once one recognizes how these models are utilized, action to change can begin. Inclusion of people with disabilities often relies on the advocacy skills of the person with the disability (McCarthy, 2007). Being an ally for disability inclusion means not waiting for someone to vocalize the problematic nature of the environment or structure in place. As an ally one might work to develop access and inclusive measures proactively rather than reactively. This requires an ally to be aware of community needs in all settings, not just when someone from the community is present. An ally can be the person who speaks out in a meeting with an informed and knowledgeable prospective that works toward inclusion. "Removing what silences them and stands in their way can tap an enormous potential of energy for change" (Johnson, 2006, p. 125). Advocacy can unravel the systems of privilege and oppression.

As a society, there is a problematic tendency to tokenize people from minority identities. For example, a classroom teacher might ask, "What about the disability perspective?" and then stare at the one person with a visible disability. This tokenizing action can be isolating and painful for the person with the disability. As an ally, one can recognize that narratives are important; however, striving for inclusion does not always mean the person with a disability (or any other minority identity) has to be the voice. As long as one speaks with information and stories of constituents on campus, you can also be a voice for inclusion, remembering the aim is to speak with members of the community not for them (Edwards, 2006).

Allies for disability can examine ways in which admission, curriculum, student services, programs, and employment (Ben-Moshe, Cory, Feldbaum, & Sagendorf, 2005; Getzel & Wehman, 2005) hold inclusive designs for people with disabilities. Re-envisioning the structures of campus removes the harmful medical and functional limitation models. The reallocation of resources does not equate to more resources, but different utilization of them to create equity. The fourth chapter discusses these aspects of the campus environment.

Conclusion

Allies promote inclusion, social change, and equity. As an ally, one must first understand one's own identities, take ownership of privilege, examine acts of oppression, and begin the journey of understanding others. Being an ally is dynamic and requires praxis: reflection, words, and action. Allies from dominant groups are essential to break the cycle of oppression, as are allies within community, given the varying sub-identities in communities. Allies on a college campus have a key role to dialogue with others about the need for inclusion through multiple modalities. Privilege and oppression will continue to have primacy in the societal structure until space for inclusion is created by visibility, voice, and equities for subordinated identity groups, including people with disabilities.

Increasing Awareness: Language, Communication Strategies, and Universally Designed Environments

> Stigmaphobia...people scrambling desperately to be included
> under the umbrella of normal—and scrambling desperately to
> cast somebody else as abnormal, crazy, abject, or disabled.
>
> Michael Bérubé (2006, p. viii)

"HAVE YOU EXCLUDED ANYONE TODAY?" When posed with this question, most professionals would agree they have included people in their daily activities. Most programs, classes, and services are intended to be inclusive and welcoming. Few professionals, if any, would intentionally exclude anyone. However, if this question is given a bit more thought, respondents might deduce that some unintentional exclusionary tactics were demonstrated in their attitudes, perceptions, and behaviors during the past week, day, or hour. Not only as a result of inaccessible physical space are people excluded, but people can also be excluded through unintentional (or possibly intentional) acts of ignoring, talking over their heads, talking about an unfamiliar subject matter, not asking for input, and even micromanaging to a point that input is not welcomed. Even though a place of business (e.g., university, organization, company, etc.) complies with the letter of the law and does not discriminate against people with disabilities per the Rehabilitation Act of 1973 (Public Law 93–112,1973), the Americans with Disabilities Act of 1990 (ADA; Public Law 101–336, 1990), and the American with

Disabilities Act Amendments Act of 2008 (Public Law 110–325, 42), have administrators and employees in some way not demonstrated the spirit of the law? For example, although an institution might obey the literal wording of the ADA guidelines (i.e., the letter of the law) by installing 36-inch wide doorways in classrooms for wheelchair access and 60-inch high signage with raised and Braille characters at classroom and office doors (Americans with Disabilities Act Accessibility Guidelines for Buildings and Facilities [ADAAG], 2002), they may not be embracing the intent or spirit of the law by providing equal access and demonstrating inclusive practices to all people with disabilities. The spirit of the law can be shown through language, communication, and responses to various situations, an example of which is universal design.

This chapter examines ways to increase awareness of people with disabilities using language and communication strategies. Insight regarding best practices for communicating with people with disabilities is addressed. This chapter also introduces and discusses universal instructional design and promotes its implementation both in and outside the classroom on college campuses. The chapter includes affirmative and negative language related to disability, communication strategies for interacting with people with various types of disabilities, and description and examples of universal design, universal instructional design, and universal design for student development.

Language of Disability

"Language empowers" (Gibson, 2011, p. 26). Language is instrumental in expressing feelings, perceptions, and attitudes. How people perceive and relate to others is reflected in language, that is, the words used to make meaning of situations. Disability language itself often offers "a symbolic and linguistic description of how individuals are to be regarded, treated, and integrated into society" (Lombana, 1989, p. 177). It is the perception of the dominant culture that defines disability, stigmatizing, and devaluing the lived experience of people with disabilities (Linton, 1998). Used as a metaphor by society, people with disabilities "have been presented as socially flawed able-bodied people, not as people with their own identities" (Ben-Moshe et al., 2005, p. 111).

Affirmative and Negative Language

Some words used to describe people with disabilities are offensive, demeaning, derogatory, and outdated. Words such as "handicapped," "vegetable," "cripple," "dumb," "crazy," and "spaz" are labels which emphasize deficit, less than, and second class. "When we use words like 'retarded,' 'lame,' or 'blind'—even if we are referring to acts or ideas and not to people at all—we perpetuate the stigma associated with disability" (Ben-Moshe et al., 2005, p. 108). In an effort to eliminate "hurt" words, recent campaigns such as *The "r" Word* (http://therword.org/) and *Spread the Word to End the Word* (http://www.r-word.org) have been launched. These words neither focus on identities nor shed light on particular characteristics, but rather may be interpreted as hurtful and hateful. Outdated and antiquated words such as "handicap" appear in older disability laws (i.e., Rehabilitation Act of 1973; Public Law 94–142, Education of All Handicapped Children Act, 1975), whereas "disability" appears in newer laws such as the ADA, ADAAA, and Individuals with Disabilities Education Act (IDEA), the latter of which is an updated version of PL94–142 and combines a children's bill of rights with federal funding (Murdick, Gartin, & Crabtree, 2007). Using current disability language demonstrates knowledge, awareness, and sensitivity to positive societal changes. Above all, it empowers. Other words or phrases that victimize individuals with disabilities include "suffering from," "afflicted with," "confined to," "stricken with," and "wheelchair bound," and labels such as "epileptic," "learning disabled," "autistic," or "the blind." Using "normal" for people without disabilities implies that the person with a disability is not normal or "abnormal," rather than a person with a specific characteristic or identity. Therefore, using the terms, "people with disabilities" and "people without disabilities" is more appropriate.

Tregoning (2009) addresses the subtleties of language and different meanings conveyed when used in-group and out-of-group. For example, words such as "gimp," "crip," and "freak" are considered acceptable when used within the disability community, indicating pride and ownership, whereas those same words are considered derogatory when used by people without disabilities. Trendy terms such as "special," "physically challenged," and "handi-capable" are neither descriptive nor accurate and should not be used (Linton, 1998). As greater numbers of individuals with disabilities take advantage of the opportunities open to them in business, industry, and travel, it becomes increasingly important to promote an environment that is positive for persons with disabilities.

One of the best and easiest ways is appropriate language use. The recommended manner is known as "person-first" language. This means that the person is emphasized first, the disability second (Myers, 2008b). Positive or affirming language places focus on the person first, then on the person's characteristic or disability. For example, "the woman who is blind" places the focus first on the person, that is, the woman, followed by the person's characteristic or identity, that is, being blind. Some other examples include the student with a learning disability, the man with cerebral palsy, the child with Down's Syndrome, the girl who uses a wheelchair, and the boy with diabetes. Various lists of terms indicating appropriate (affirmative) language and negative language (i.e., terms to avoid) have been distributed over the years (e.g., City of San Antonio Department of Public Works, 2011; http://www.easterseals.com; Clinton & Higbee, 2011; as well as the "Communication Tips" section of this monograph) and can be found on various websites located in the references.

In *Claiming Disability*, Linton (1998) describes how she progressed from negatively descriptive words of disability purporting the medical model such as handicapped, crippled, and lame to person-first language, focusing on the person first, then addressing the person's disability. Linton used person-first language in her early years or teaching. Years later, while becoming more involved in the disability rights movement, she began to see person-first language as avoidance and began describing herself as a "disabled" woman. Linton makes a strong argument that the common terminology used in discussing people with disabilities assigns a deficit identity to the disability population and obstructs societal change:

> It was around this time, somewhere in the early '90s, that I also
> began to use the term 'disabled woman' to identify myself. I no
> longer said, 'I am a woman with a disability'; instead I was
> likely to describe myself by forefronting disability. 'I am a disabled

woman,' I would say, and then might explain to my students, 'That means that I identify as a member of the minority group—disabled people—and that is a strong influence on my cultural make-up, who I am, and the way that I think.' (Linton, 2007, p. 118)

Disability language varies from person to person and certainly can be based on individual preferences and philosophies. Person-first language is one way to focus on the person instead of the disability, providing an inclusive way to communicate about one of the multiple identities of human beings.

Communication Strategies

In addition to using appropriate and affirming language, behavior and non-verbal communication send messages indicating our thoughts, feelings, and perceptions toward people with disabilities. Over the years, various authors and educators have provided recommended techniques for communicating with people with disabilities. Popular publications include those by national associations such as the American Council for the Blind, DEAF Inc., Leaning Disabilities Association, the National Autism Association, and others publications by independent living centers, local nonprofit organizations, free-lance consultants, and disability services departments at colleges and universities. Inclusive communication shows respect, comfort, and awareness, that is, treating others as you would like to be treated—treating everyone as first-class citizens (Gibson, 2006; Myers, 2009b; Myers, Spudich, Spudich, & Laux, 2012; Tregoning, 2009). Interacting comfortably with people with and without disabilities is the key to effective communication and understanding. Some recommendations for communicating with people with disabilities include the following:

- Speak directly to a person with a disability. Because an individual has a functional limitation, it does not mean the individual cannot communicate for himself/herself.

- Speak in a regular tone. There is no need to shout at a person with a disability. A physical or cognitive limitation does not mean the person cannot hear you or understand you.
- Use descriptive language indicating direction or size when communicating with people with cognitive and visual disabilities. Instead of saying, "over here," "that way," and "this big," use words to describe the direction, space, length, and size (e.g., "about two feet to your left," "straight ahead," "two inches from the curb," etc.).
- Identify yourself when you meet a person with a visual disability. In groups, identify to whom you are speaking and notify people when it is their turn to speak.
- Describe what is drawn, written, or illustrated during presentations. When you ask people to read it on their own, you are excluding those who are not able to see or read it.
- Treat adults as adults. Having disabilities does not mean people are children or less than. Treat them as you would anyone else.
- Listen attentively to people with speech disabilities. Do not assume you understand or pretend you understand. Ask for clarification as needed.
- It is always appropriate to offer your help; just do not assume the person will need or accept your help.

In disability awareness sessions conducted by the authors of this monograph, people continually ask questions about what to say, how it say it, what to do, what is appropriate, and what is offensive. To answer some of these questions, the authors are including the following "Communication Tips" for interactions with people with visual, hearing, mobility, and cognitive disabilities. Although there are many more suggestions available, these are some of the most common communication strategies recommended for interactions with this population.

Communication Tips

In order to decrease inappropriate and potentially even offensive interactions with people with disabilities, the authors suggest utilizing the following communication tips.

When You Meet a Person With a Visual Disability

- It is always appropriate to offer your help; just do not be surprised if the individual would "rather do it myself."
- If you are helping and not sure what to do, ask the person.
- A gentle touch on the elbow will indicate to a person with a visual disability that you are speaking to him/her.
- If you are walking with a person who is blind, do not take that person's arm; rather let that person take your arm.
- Do not shout. "Blind" does not mean hard of hearing.
- If you have a question for the person with a visual disability, ask him/her, not his/her companion. "Blind" does not mean one cannot speak.
- Never pet a guide dog, except when the dog is "off-duty." Even then you should ask the dog's master first.
- Do not worry about substituting words for "see," "look," or even "blind." Do not avoid them where these words fit. You can talk about blindness itself, when you both feel comfortable about it.
- When you meet a person you know with a visual disability, mention your name. It is difficult to recognize voices unless you happen to have a very distinctive one.

When You Meet a Person Who Is Deaf or Hard of Hearing

- Speak clearly and distinctly, but do not exaggerate. Use normal speed unless asked to slow down.
- Provide a clear view of your mouth. Waving your hands or holding something in front of your lips, thus hiding them, makes lip reading impossible. Do not chew gum.
- Use a normal tone unless you are asked to raise your voice. Shouting will be of no help.
- Speak directly to the person, rather than from the side or back of the person.
- Speak expressively. Because persons who are deaf cannot hear subtle changes in tone, which may indicate sarcasm or seriousness, many will rely on your facial expressions, gestures, and body language to understand you.

- If you are having trouble understanding the speech of a person who is deaf, feel free to ask him/her to repeat. If that does not work, then use a paper and pen.
- If a person who is deaf is with an interpreter, speak directly to the person who is deaf—not to the interpreter.

When You Meet a Person With a Mobility Disability

- Offer help, but wait until it is accepted before giving it. Giving help before it is accepted is rude and sometimes can be unsafe.
- Accept the fact that a disability exists. Not acknowledging a disability is similar to ignoring someone's gender or height. But to ask personal questions regarding the disability would be inappropriate until a closer relationship develops in which personal questions are more naturally asked.
- Talk directly to a person with a disability. Because an individual has a functional limitation, it does not mean the individual cannot communicate for himself/herself.
- Do not park your car in a parking place that is specially designed for use by a person with a disability. These are reserved out of necessity, not convenience.
- Treat a person with a disability as a healthy person. Because an individual has a functional limitation, it does not mean the individual is sick.
- Keep in mind that persons with disabilities have the same activities of daily living as you do.

When You Meet a Person With a Cognitive Disability

- Use very clear, specific language.
- Condense lengthy directions into steps.
- Use short, concise instructions.
- Present verbal information at a relatively slow pace, with appropriate pauses for processing time and with repetition if necessary.
- Provide cues to help with transitions: "In five minutes we'll be going to lunch."
- Reinforce information with pictures or other visual images.
- Use modeling, rehearsing, and role-playing.

- Use concrete rather than abstract language.
- Limit the use of sarcasm or subtle humor.
- If you are not sure what to do or say, just ask the person what he/she needs.

Universally Designed Environments

Designing accessible environments is essential on college campuses and in the community. People with and without disabilities benefit from accessible buildings, walkways, transportation, programs, and services. By applying universal design principles to campus facilities, college curriculum, and student life, the entire campus community will be able to experience all aspects of the institution.

Universal Design

Eliminating barriers, promoting inclusion, and recognizing and appreciating the lived experience of people with disabilities are the essence of the social constructive model of disability. Inclusion of all people means providing access to all people with as few accommodations as possible. Case in point: How do all people access a sidewalk from the street? Whether walking, riding a bike, using a wheelchair, using crutches, pushing a stroller, or pulling a rolling suitcase, all people should be able to move comfortably over a curb. Therefore, architects created the universally designed curb cut, an indentation in a curb with a specified slope that allows all people equal access to both the sidewalk and the street. The architectural term known as "universal design" (UD) was conceptualized by Ronald L. Mace as "the designing of all products and the built environment to be aesthetic and usable to the greatest extent possible by everyone, regardless of their age, ability, or status in life" (Center for Universal Design, 2010, para. 2). According to the Center for Universal Design at North Carolina State University, the following seven principles are the foundation of UD: (a) *equitable use*: the design is useful and marketable to people with diverse abilities; (b) *flexibility in use*: the design accommodates a wide range of individual preferences and abilities; (c) *simple and intuitive use*: use of the design is easy to understand, regardless of the user's experience, knowledge, language skills, or current concentration level; (d) *perceptible information*: the design communicates necessary information effectively to the user, regardless of ambient conditions or the user's sensory abilities; (e) *tolerance for error*: the design minimizes hazards and the adverse consequences of accidental or unintended actions; (f) *low physical effort*: the design can be used efficiently, comfortably, and with a minimum of fatigue; and (g) *size and space for approach and use*: appropriate size and space is provided for approach, reach, manipulation, and use, regardless of the user's body size, posture, or mobility (Center for Universal Design, 2001).

In addition to the curb cut described above, other common examples of universal design of facilities are the automatic door, closed captioning, and audible streetlights. Traditionally used in airports, grocery stores, and hospitals, automatic doors are now used in many office structures, academic buildings, retail establishments, and day-care facilities. Closed captioning, which provides written text for audible words in movies, television shows, and videos, is a federally mandated accommodation and a standard specification on all analog televisions produced or sold in the United States beginning July 1993 and on all digital televisions as of July 2002 (Federal Communications Commission, Consumer Guide, 2012). The audible street crossing light is yet another example of UD. In addition to a light that changes color from red to green, the words "walk" and "don't walk" appear together with a picture of a person walking and not walking accompanied by the audible words "Walk"/"Don't Walk" or another audible sound such as a bell chime or chirping bird to indicate when it is appropriate to cross the street.

Universal Instructional Design

Following the concept of universal design of facilities, educators brought UD into the classroom. Over the past 20 years, much has been written about universal design in higher education, also known as "universal instructional design" (UID), "universal design of instruction" (UDI) when applied to instruction, and "universal design for learning" (UDL) when applied to learning

(Burgstahler & Cory, 2008; Higbee & Goff, 2008; McGuire, Scot, & Shaw, 2006). Universal design was applied to education, particularly to higher education, through several federally funded projects at the University of Minnesota, University of Washington, and the University of Connecticut, among others. Each of these institutions conducted research and provided training and development on universal design initiatives in postsecondary education settings. Using the principles of universal design, these projects offered standards for best practice. Fox, Hatfield, and Collins (2003) and Johnson and Fox (2003) address UD and UID guiding principles based on Chickering and Gamson's (1987) best practices for undergraduate education. These principles are as follows: (a) creating respectful welcoming environments; (b) determining the essential components of a course or program; (c) communicating class/program expectations; (d) providing constructive feedback; (e) exploring the use of natural supports for learning, including technology, to enhance opportunities for all learners; (f) designing teaching/instructional methods that consider diverse learning styles, abilities, ways of knowing, and previous experience and background knowledge; (g) creating multiple ways for students/employees to demonstrate their knowledge; and (h) promoting interaction among and between faculty and students, and employers and employees (p. 2).

The term "universal instructional design" (UID) was originally coined by Silver, Bourke, and Strehorn (1998). Some examples of UID in curriculum include reaching out to students prior to the first day of class; learning students' names; putting syllabi and reading lists online; providing all print materials including websites and emails in readable high-contrast sans serif font; captioning videos; offering study guides and support systems; and creating multiple modes of teaching and learning such as traditional lecture, discussion, and tests mixed with the "flipped classroom" (i.e., online teaching sessions with face-to-face application) and social media activities. UID principles such as respectful, welcoming environments, timely feedback, accessible instructional materials, and comfortable interactions may benefit people with and without disabilities. For students, it eliminates the need to be segregated for accommodations, it addresses the stigma associated with medical model (i.e., disability as deficiency), it recognizes individual differences among all learners, including in learning styles and ways of knowing, and it enables students to use their strengths. For faculty, administrators and staff, using UID practices is cost-effective, time-efficient, enhances student engagement, and reduces the need for last-minute modifications to accommodate students with a variety of needs, including but not limited to students with disabilities. Created initially for individuals with disabilities, UID has been expanded to address access for people whose native language is not English and for people of various cultures, ethnicities, ages, and learning styles. An expanded model of UID, integrated multicultural instructional design (IMID) is under development (Barajas & Higbee, 2003; Higbee & Barajas, 2007; Higbee, Goff, & Schultz, 2012; Higbee, Schultz, & Goff, 2010). "IMID picks up where UID leaves off, adding explorations of what we teach to the UID model that already addresses how we teach, how we support learning, and how we assess learning" (Higbee, 2012, para. 16).

Universal Design for Student Development

As UID became more widespread both inside and outside of the classroom, Higbee and her colleagues extended UID to student affairs personnel and their functional areas. Coining the phrase, "universal design for student development" (UDSD), Higbee and Goff (2008) describe the concept and provide examples for practice in their book, *Pedagogy and Student Services for Institutional Transformation* (PASS IT), and its accompanying guidebooks (Goff & Higbee, 2008a, 2008b), produced by a national team of faculty, staff, and administrators via a federally funded project (http://cehd.umn.edu/passit). Checklists are included in the guidebooks to assess for UID and UDSD practices by faculty, student development practitioners, and student leaders. (These checklists are included in the educational materials developed through PASS IT and can also be accessed at http://cte.slu.edu/ui.)

When developing services and planning events and activities, Higbee (2008) recommended posing the following questions:

- *"How can we ensure that everyone who wants to participate will have the opportunity to do so?*

- *What steps can we take to ensure that everyone will feel included?*
- *What do we need to do to ensure that everyone will benefit to the greatest extent possible?" (p. 200)*

Implementing intentional UDSD practices, practitioners and student leaders will provide accessible programs and services:

> *Not only is it important to model best practices of UID in our work as professionals on campus, but it is also important to advise student leaders to incorporate UID within their leadership roles in campus groups, organizations, and teams. One way student leaders can immediately have an impact on campus is to promote open access to all other students. (Lindburg, 2012, para. 8)*

Examples of such practices include ensuring all activities, events, and meetings are in accessible, welcoming locations; supporting written announcements and materials with online and audio versions; promoting accessible (i.e., screen reader and low vision friendly) websites, online registrations, surveys, and other web-based student information sites; captioning videos; and utilizing high-contrast sans serif font on publications, promotional materials, and other print media.

Commitment from national, regional, and state associations to adopt UD, UID, and UDSD principles is a major step toward acceptance and common practice. One association in particular has demonstrated this commitment. ACPA College Students International has offered UID webinars, programs, workshops, and presentations. Articles on universal design and inclusion have been published in the *Journal of College Student Development* and *About Campus*, both ACPA publications. *Making Good on the Promise: Student Affairs Professionals with Disabilities* (Higbee & Mitchell, 2009) is sponsored by the ACPA Standing Committee on Disability and contains articles and first-person accounts from over 20 of its members who are professionals with disabilities and their allies. For three years, the association hosted *Allies for Inclusion: The Ability Exhibit*, a national traveling exhibit that promotes disability awareness and inclusion, including UD, UID, UDSD, person-first language, and communication strategies. The ACPA Governing Board and Foundation Board promote the use of inclusive language and the production of UID-friendly web pages and print media. The association's most recent initiative was a four-part series published in *ACPA Developments*. In "Expanding the Frame: Applying Universal Design in Higher Education," ACPA Standing Committee on Disability members Thompson (2012), Myers (2012), Lindburg (2012), and Higbee (2012) describe their personal experiences with UID as an administrator, a faculty member, a disability services provider, and a professional with a disability. The purpose of the series was to provide a standard framework in which to develop learning environments in the association and beyond. ACPA is just one example of an association's commitment to disability education and inclusion. It serves as a model for other associations to emulate.

Conclusion

Increasing awareness through language, communication strategies, and universal design principles promotes the inclusion of people with disabilities and provides professionals with the tools to shift the disability paradigm and relearn misinformation. The issues encountered by people with disabilities are not consequences of their disabilities; rather they are "products of interaction between the social and built environment" (Longmore, 2003, p. 2). Recognizing and respecting the identities of others can be demonstrated through respectful communication. Higbee (2012) encourages us to avoid labeling people on the basis of a single aspect of their social identity (think "person-first"); ask people what terms they prefer to describe aspects of their social identity; refrain from using "othering" language (e.g., *normal* and *regular*); and be aware that some identity groups are "reclaiming" language to refer to themselves (e.g., *fag*, *crip*, *girl*, and *trannie*), but "[t]he subtleties of language become more difficult when the same words spoken in-group hold a different meaning when used out-of-group" (Tregoning, 2009, p. 174).

Educators are models for inclusion. When addressing language, culture, and climate, ask students to reflect on times when they have been the targets of oppressive language and communication. Discuss potential reactions to oppressive language used by others, including when presented as humor. Use these reflections and discussions to create role-playing activities, and encourage students to follow our lead in being allies in respectful language use, comfortable interactions, and creative universal design techniques, thus becoming allies for inclusion.

The New Movement in Disability Education and Advocacy

What you are is where you were when … AGAIN!
Dr. Morris Massey (Enterprise Media, 2006)

The Disability Movement of the 1960s was filled with protest marches, sit-ins, banners, and activists. Voices were raised and heard and laws were passed. The term "disability movement" calls to mind images of bus protests, people leaving wheelchairs to crawl up the Capitol steps, and individuals with a multitude of disabilities banning together for a common cause—equal rights of persons with disabilities. So, what does the disability movement look like today? What is the new movement in disability rights and inclusion? How do you envision it? What can be done to promote it? This chapter offers current strategies to address inequity for people with disabilities and identify gaps and ongoing challenges to ensure inclusion.

A New Vision for Disability

The disability paradigm is shifting. Educators and advocates of disability are directing attention away from the medical model that concentrates on deficit, defect, and illness, focusing on the person's body and its limitations. Instead, they are moving toward the lived experiences of people with disabilities and the social construction of disability in today's society. Awareness of disability issues is increasing with the passage of disability legislation (e.g., the

Americans with Disabilities Act of 1990 [ADA], the Americans with Disabilities Act Amendments Act [ADAAA] of 2008, the 21st Century Communications and Accessibility Act of 2010 [CVAA], etc.) and more public attention is given to disability rights and responsibilities in the areas of employment, education, government, public accommodations, transportation, and technology. Such public attention is accompanied by the assumption that most Americans are aware of laws prohibiting discrimination against people with disabilities. Most people recognize in the scope of their occupation that the letter of the law must be followed. The hundreds of court cases related to disability, some mentioned in this monograph, inform and remind us of the legal ramifications for not complying with the law. Despite recent legislation and legal action, marginalization and exclusion remain in many people's minds and behaviors. To counteract this mentality, various national and local efforts are attempting to "change the tide" and shift the attention and actions to the spirit of the law. "A new vision of disability education that moves away from a limitations framework ... emphasizes the humanizing of disabilities. These attitudes of respect, comfort, and awareness readily map to learning outcomes espoused by many colleges and universities" (Myers, 2009a, p. 18). By incorporating universal instructional design and disability education into the curriculum and intentionally designing opportunities for students to demonstrate inclusion, learning outcomes may be achieved:

> *Even for those of us who have always been very intentional and reflective in our work, UID has simultaneously broadened and focused our thinking. We think more broadly about the diversity of our students and how students' social identities can shape their learning experiences, and meanwhile we are also more focused on how we can ensure that no students are excluded or marginalized.* (Goff & Higbee, 2008c, p. 2)

The social inequities for people with disabilities remain problematic. The theoretical models to view and address disability paired the attitudes of individuals in society remain in a cyclical, deleterious pattern for the disability community. Strides to confront the systemic inequities are necessary in order to change the marginalization that occurs. The systemic challenges trickle down into institutions of higher education, where social stratification negatively impacts people with disabilities.

The near absence of disability education in the curriculum reinforces the negative societal attitude toward disability. Disability is often invisible even in conversations of social identities. A counternarrative can be provided in educational curriculum in a variety of ways to shift perceptions of disability from negative or flawed to embracing and acceptance. There is a need to have open communication and dialogue about disability in order to remove the stigma. This will assist with challenging the normative views and environments that have been constructed which do not account for people with disabilities. The content of the curriculum and the access to the content are both factors to consider in the challenge of reshaping the curriculum (Conner & Baglieri, 2009). Inclusive pedagogical approach to disability should be implemented in the classroom across disciplines. One-time "events tend to re-inscribe pity, fear, discomfort, and misunderstanding of disability, particularly for abled participants" (Conner & Baglieri, 2009, p. 348) that is counterproductive to the educational aims. Instead, integration of disability as an interwoven topic in course curriculum allows for a consistent deconstruction of the silenced societal disability narrative. Additionally, integration throughout course content allows for a deeper understanding of disability.

Intersectional identities with disability have not thoroughly been explored. The richness of voice, inquiry into intersections of disability identities can provide, would serve valuable in the larger understanding of the experience of people with disabilities. Exploring the intersections disarms the societal normative views of people with disabilities. Understanding the unique intersections can provide inclusion and access for people with disabilities in communities currently propagating identity from a limited mainstream marginalized voice. Rhetoric of difference provides writing to learn and writing to communicate (Bridwell-Bowles, 1998) that can be valuable for those within community and those working to reframe ones hegemonic, privilege promoting frames.

Campus ecology (Strange & Banning, 2001) must be examined through the lens of disability. Currently, the vast lack of thoughtfulness for access and inclusion of people with disabilities provides a narrative that disability is invisible until people are forced to confront the issue due to required access laws or individual requests. Examining human aggregate, physical, organizational, and social climate will assist with deconstructing the current environments, provide strong critique of those environments, and allow for intentional rebuilding through inclusive practices. Evaluating the interactions between people with disabilities and their environments offers a perspective to address the power of influences on self-efficacy, student learning, and conditions for student success at an institution.

Education Curriculum

The development of the field of disability studies is changing the way people think, perceive, and learn about disability. Operating through a minority model lens, this recent field of study in higher education uses an interdisciplinary approach to focus on the lived experiences of people with disabilities while deconstructing the stereotypes, myths, and assumptions created by society. The Society for Disability Studies (SDS) "promotes the study of disability social, cultural, and political contexts … [and] seeks to augment understanding of disability in all cultures and historical periods, to promote greater awareness of the experiences of disabled people, and to advocate for social change" (SDS, 2013, para. 1). Disability studies programs are being developed and offered at many universities throughout the United States. Research and scholarship focusing on multiple identities and the intersection of identities, such as McRuer's (2006) "Crip Theory" focusing on queerness and disability, address the concept of the global body through a sociopolitical lens.

Inclusion Initiatives

The list of recent educational initiatives demonstrating the spirit of the law (some of which have been described earlier in this monograph) is rapidly growing. In addition to PASS IT at the University of Minnesota and DO-IT at the University of Washington (described previously), other initiatives include the *Spread the Word to End the Word* campaign, the National Service Inclusion Project, Everyone Matters, and *Allies for Inclusion: The Ability Exhibit*. Brief descriptions of these follow.

Spread the Word to End the Word (http://www.r-word.org) is a campaign which hopes to end the use of the "R" word, that is, retarded. When the term mental retardation was originally introduced, it was a medical diagnosis. From the clinical terms, the words retard and retarded were formed to negatively describe and degrade individuals with intellectual disabilities. Too often these words have become common language by individuals without disabilities as synonyms for dumb and stupid. These terms may seem trivial to some, but can cause people with intellectual disabilities to feel stereotyped and feel less valued. The campaign asks individuals to pledge not to use the "R" word and provides opportunities for individuals to get involved with organizations like the Special Olympics and Best Buddies.

The National Service Inclusion Project (NSIP) (http://www.serviceandinclusion.org) encourages the active engagement of all people, regardless of their abilities, in community service efforts. NSIP is a resource to individuals who want to provide staff training on disability inclusion. NSIP provides information regarding outreach and recruitment of potential volunteers with disabilities, appropriate language concerning individuals with disabilities, and training on accessibility, design, and legal responsibilities. The National Service Inclusion Project prides itself on helping to create meaningful service opportunities for all individuals.

Everyone Matters 2012 (http://everyonematters2012.com) is the newest initiative from the *What's Your Issue Foundation*. What's Your Issue sponsors an annual youth film competition called Film Your Issue with celebrities George Clooney and Anderson Cooper involved in the judging and selection of winners. Everyone Matters is broadening the impact of the What's Your Issue Foundation by providing new outlets for individuals to raise awareness for issues they support. By using social media and user-generated content, Everyone Matters hopes to spread the word about important social justice issues and encourages users to join the "Don't Judge" campaign.

Allies for Inclusion: The Ability Exhibit Project (http://www.slu.edu/theabilityexhibit) comprises three initiatives: a Traveling Edition, a Workshop Edition, and a K–12 Edition. Created from a Saint Louis University graduate student's class project in 2010, this award-winning multimedia interactive exhibit is hosted by colleges and universities from coast to coast. Through donor and grant support, age-level activities are being developed for elementary and secondary education students to promote respect for people with disabilities, develop comfort during interactions, and raise awareness for becoming allies for inclusion.

The New Look of Disability

Media attention toward celebrities with disabilities is raising public awareness. Personal stories of celebrities, such as Olympians Im Dong Hyun and Natalia Partyka; Ironman champion, Jason Lester; national champion surfer, Bethany Hamilton; Oscar-winning actor, Michael J. Fox; Grammy winner and Soul Hall-of-Famer, Stevie Wonder; college professor and author, Dr. Temple Grandin; and Paralympic athlete and model, Aimee Mullins, shift stereotypical views of weakness to absolute perceptions of strength. Thoughts of what people with disabilities *cannot* do are being replaced with certainties of what they *can* do. Television shows and movies depict individuals with disabilities on a regular basis, from Artie in *Glee* to Nemo and Dory in *Finding Nemo* to Sheldon in *Big Bang Theory*. People with disabilities "can now become the architects of their own identities and indeed continue to change those identities by designing their bodies from a place of empowerment" (Mullins, 2009, TED Talks).

A Personal Call to Action

Now is the time for everyone to become architects of our own identities. What can be done in our own lives, on our campuses, and in our communities to humanize disability? How can the lived experiences of people with disabilities be recognized, and what can be done to create allies of inclusion? Below are a few ideas.

Use pop culture. Turn campus movies into social justice opportunities. Choose documentaries or films, which may evoke controversial topics and provide an opportunity for students to discuss the issues after the film. Turn a cultural performance that may already exist on campus (such as a Mexican fiesta or Hawaiian Lau) into a learning opportunity by asking individuals from these cultures to discuss oppression or marginalization they may have faced during their lifetime.

Take an oath. Start an Oath of Inclusion on your campus. Encourage students to sign an oath or pledge, which says they will not discriminate their peers and will promote inclusion within their communities and organizations on campus. *Allies for Inclusion: The Ability Exhibit* ends with participants signing an "I Pledge to be an Ally" poster, which becomes the property of the host institution. *Spread the Word to End the Word* offers an online pledge that only takes a click of the mouse to sign.

Role play, model, and discuss language, communication both inside and outside the classroom. Create a campus-wide diversity committee and a student organization for students with disabilities and their allies to advocate for social justice.

Add to the body of knowledge in the area of disability through research and scholarship, which connects directly with people with disabilities. Consider multiple identities and the cross-section of these identities as they relate to cultural, social, and political contexts.

These are only a few of the many ways to create inclusive experiences for students. "Whether operating in the classroom, in a cocurricular program or through a learning community, disability education, as envisioned here, creates a respectful, welcoming environment and relies on allies to support and advocate for the social justice of persons with disabilities" (Myers, 2009a, p. 20).

A Global Call to Action

Disability is a human condition. As such, it logically is a part of diversity. Disability not only exists in the United States and in American education but also in all parts of the world. It should be in the minds and hearts of educators throughout the globe. Article 24 of the United Nations (UN, 2006)

Convention on the Rights of Persons With Disabilities states that an inclusive education must be provided at all levels and that all faculty and staff must be trained to provide this inclusive education:

> *Nations throughout the world have signed the United Nations (UN) Convention on the Rights of Persons with Disabilities. Many postsecondary educators support the ideals of access and equity for students with disabilities, but have received no training in how to ensure that these goals are achieved. (Duranczyk, Myers, Couillard, Schoen, & Higbee, 2013, p. 63)*

Education and training for faculty, staff, and administrators in elementary, secondary, and postsecondary institutions is essential in order to create accessible curriculum and facilities for all students. The intention of this monograph was to fill in some of the gaps in that professional development process. This monograph provides some background information of disability in the United States, offers a profile of current college students with disabilities, encourages and describes the development of allies, and introduces the concepts of universal design, universal instructional design, and universal design for student development, which connect disability to the larger agendas for equity, access, and inclusion. As recommended by the UN (2006) Convention, the incorporation of universal design practices will eliminate the need for most individual accommodations, thus providing equal access for all. Access then moves from a disability issue focusing on functional limitations of individuals to a multicultural approach of inclusion involving people of various ages, races, ethnicities, languages, and abilities.

Morris Massey (Enterprise Media, 1972) reminds us in the first line of this monograph, "*What you are is where you were when.*" As faculty, staff, and administrators, it is our responsibility to design today what future generations remember as they create their own identities. It is our responsibility to be their allies for equity, access, and inclusion.

References

Abes, E. S., Jones, S. R., & McEwen, M. (2007). Reconceptualizing the model of multiple dimensions of identity: The role of meaning-making capacity in the construction of multiple identities. *Journal of College Student Development, 48,* 1–22.

American Council on Education (ACE). (2008). *Serving those who serve: Higher education and America's veterans.* Retrieved October 11, 2013, from http://www.acenet.edu/news-room/Pages/Georgetown-Summit.aspx

Americans with Disabilities Act of 1990, 42 U.S.C.A. § 12101 *et seq* (1990). Retrieved August 6, 2011, from http://www.ada.gov/pubs/ada.htm

Americans with Disabilities Act (ADA) Accessibility Guidelines for Buildings and Facilities (ADAAG). (2002). *ADA Standards.* Washington, DC: United States Architectural and Transportation Barriers Compliance Board. Retrieved February 28, 2013, from http://www.access-board.gov/guidelines-and-standards/buildings-and-sites/about-the-ada-standards/ada-standards

Americans with Disabilities Act Amendments Act of 2008, Public Law 110–325, 42 U.S.C. § 12102 (2008). Retrieved August 6, 2011, from http://www.law.georgetown.edu/archiveada/documents/ADAAACR9.17.08.pdf

Asch, A. (1984). The experience of disability: A challenge for psychology. *American Psychologist, 39,* 529–536.

Asch, A., & Fine, M. (1988). Introduction: Beyond pedestals. In M. Fine & A. Asch (Eds.), *Women with disabilities: Essays in psychology, culture, and politics* (pp. 1–37). Philadelphia, PA: Temple University Press.

Association for Higher Education and Disability (AHEAD). (2012). Retrieved February 27, 2013, from http://www.ahead.org

Bandura, A. (1977). Toward a unifying theory of behavior change. *Psychological Review, 84,* 191–215.

Barajas, H. L., & Higbee, J. L. (2003). Where do we go from here? Universal design as a model for multicultural education. In J. L. Higbee (Ed.), *Curriculum transformation and disability: Implementing universal design in higher education* (pp. 285–290). Minneapolis: Center for Research on Developmental Education and Urban Literacy, University of Minnesota.

Baxter Magolda, M. (1999). Defining and redefining student learning. In E. Whitt (Ed.), *Student learning as student affairs work.* NASPA Monograph Series 23 (pp. 35–49). Washington, DC: National Association of Student Personnel Administrators.

Bell, L. A. (1997). Theoretical foundations for social justice. In M. Adams, L. A. Bell, & P. Griffin (Eds.), *Teaching for diversity and social justice: A sourcebook* (pp. 1–14). New York, NY: Routledge Press.

Ben-Moshe, L., Cory, R. C., Feldbaum, M., & Sagendorf, K. (2005). *Building pedagogical curb cuts: Incorporating disability in the university classroom and curriculum.* Syracuse, NY: The Graduate School, Syracuse University.

Bérubé, M. (2006). Foreword. In R. McRuer (Ed.), *Cultural signs of queerness and disability* (pp. vii–xi). New York: New York University Press.

Bishop, A. (2002). *Becoming an ally: Breaking the cycle of oppression—in people* (2nd ed.). Halifax, Nova Scotia, Canada: Fernwood.

Boyer, E. L. (1990). *In search of community.* Princeton, NJ: The Carnegie Foundation for the Advancement of Teaching.

Brault, M. W. (2012, July). *Americans with disabilities: 2010.* Current Population Reports. Washington, DC: United States Census Bureau.

Bridwell-Bowles, L. (1998). *Identity matters: Rhetorics of difference.* Upper Saddle River, NJ: Prentice-Hall.

Brinckerhoff, L. C., Shaw, S. F., & McGuire, J. M. (1992). Promoting access, accommodations, and independence for college students with learning disabilities. *Journal of Learning Disabilities, 25,* 417–429.

Broido, E. M. (2000). The development of social justice allies during college: A phenomenological investigation. *Journal of College Student Development, 41,* 3–18.

Bryan, A., & Myers, K. (2006). Students with disabilities: Doing what's right. *About Campus, 2*(4), 18–22.

Burgstahler, S. E., & Cory, R. C. (Eds.). (2008). *Universal design in higher education: From principles to practice.* Cambridge, MA: Harvard Education Press.

Burnett, S. E., & Segoria, J. (2009). Collaboration for military transition students from combat to college: It takes a community. *Journal of Postsecondary Education and Disability, 22*(1), 233–238.

Business and Legal Resources (BLR). (2013). *ADA.* Retrieved February 14, 2013, from http://www.blr.com/hrtips/ada

Casey-Powell, D., & Souma, A. (2009). Allies in our midst. In J. Higbee & A. Mitchell (Eds.), *Making good on the promise: Student affairs professionals with disabilities* (pp. 149–170). Washington, DC: American College Personnel Association, University Press of America.

Cass, V. C. (1979). Homosexual identity formation: A theoretical model. *Journal of Homosexuality, 4*(3), 219–235.

Castaneda, R., & Peters, M. L. (2000). Ableism. In M. Adams, W. J. Blumenfeld, R. Castaneda, H. W. Hackmand, M. L. Peters, & X. Zuniga (Eds.), *Readings for diversity and social justice: An anthology on racism, anti-Semitism, sexism, heterosexism, ableism, and classism* (pp. 319–323). New York, NY: Routledge Press.

Center for Universal Design. (2001). *The principles of universal design* (Version 2.0). Retrieved February 28, 2013, from http://www.ncsu.edu/ncsu/design/cud/about_ud/udprinciples.htm

Center for Universal Design. (2010). *Ronald L. Mace.* Retrieved February 28, 2013, from http://www.ncsu.edu/ncsu/design/cud/about_us/usronmace.htm

Chickering, A. W., & Gamson, Z. F. (1987). Seven principles for good practice in undergraduate education. *AAHE Bulletin, 39*(7), 3–7.

Civil Rights Act of 1964, 42 U.S.C.A. § 2000e *et seq.* (1964). Retrieved February 28, 2013, from http://www.eeoc.gov/laws/statutes/titlevii.cfm

City of San Antonio Department of Public Works. (2011). *2011 disability etiquette handbook.* Retrieved December 6, 2013, from http://www.sanantonio.gov/publicworks/dao/etiquettehandbook2011.aspx

Clinton, L., & Higbee, J. L. (2011). The invisible hand: The power of creating welcoming postsecondary learning experiences. *Journal of College Teaching and Learning, 8*(5), 11–16.

Cohen, A. (2004). Test anxiety and its effect on students with learning disabilities. *Learning Disability Quarterly, 27,* 186–184.

Conner, D. J., & Baglieri, S. (2009). Tipping the scales: Disability studies asks "how much diversity can you take?" In S. R. Steinberg (Ed.), *Diversity and multiculturalism: A reader* (pp. 341–362). New York, NY: Peter Lang.

Council for the Advancement of Standards in Higher Education (CAS). (2012). *Disability services and resources.* Retrieved February 28, 2013, from http://www.cas.edu/index.php/index.php/index.php

Cross, W. E. (1995). The psychology of nigrescence: Revising the Cross model. In J. G. Ponterotto, J. M. Casas, L. A. Suzuki, & C. M. Alexander (Eds.), *Handbook of multicultural counseling* (pp. 93–122). Thousand Oaks, CA: Sage.

Disability Access Consultants (DAC). (2012). *Five titles of the ADA.* Retrieved February 16, 2013, from http://www.adaconsultants.com/ADATitles.aspx

Doe v. New York University, 511 F. Supp. 606 (1981).

Doherty v. Southern College of Optometry, 862 F.2d 570 (1988).

Duranczyk, I. M., Myers, K. A., Couillard, E. K., Schoen, S., & Higbee, J. L. (2013). Enacting the spirit of the United Nations convention on the rights of persons with disabilities: The role of postsecondary faculty in ensuring access. *Journal of Diversity Management, 8*(2), 63–72.

Edwards, K. E. (2006). Aspiring social justice ally identity development. *NASPA Journal, 43*(4), 39–60.

Edwards, K. E., & Jones, S. R. (2009). Putting my man face on: A grounded theory of college men's gender identity development. *Journal of College Student Development, 50*(2), 210–228.

Ellison, R. W. (1952). *Invisible man.* New York, NY: Random House.

Enterprise Media. (Producer). (1972). *What you are is where you were when* [DVD]. Retrieved October 8, 2013, from http://www.enterprisemedia.com/product/00127/

Enterprise Media. (Producer). (2006). *What you are is where you where when...Again!* [DVD]. Retrieved October 8, 2013, from http://www.enterprisemedia.com/product/00125/

Evans, N. J. (2008). Theoretical foundations of universal instructional design. In J. L. Higbee & E. Goff (Eds.), *Pedagogy and student services for institutional transformation: Implementing universal design in higher education* (pp. 11–23). Minneapolis: University of Minnesota Press.

Evans, N. J., Assadi, J., & Herriott, T. (2005). Encouraging the development of disability allies. In R. D. Reason, E. M. Broido, T. L. Davis, & N. J. Evans (Eds.), *New Directions for Student Services: No. 110. Developing social justice allies* (pp. 67–79). San Francisco, CA: Jossey-Bass.

Evans, N. J., & Herriott, T. (2009). Philosophical and theoretical approaches to disability. In J. Higbee & A. Mitchell (Eds.), *Making good on the promise: Student affairs professionals with disabilities* (pp. 27–40). Washington, DC: American College Personnel Association and University Press of America.

Evans, N. J., Herriott, T. K., & Myers, K. A. (2009). Integrating disability into the framework in the training of student affairs professionals. In A. Mitchell & J. Higbee (Eds.), *Making good on the promise: Student affairs professionals with disabilities* (pp. 111–128). Lanham, MD: University Press of America.

Fassinger, R. E. (1998). Lesbian, gay, and bisexual identity and student development theory. In R. L. Sanlow (Ed.), *Working with lesbian, say, bisexual, and transgender college students* (pp. 13–22). Westport, CT: Greenwood Press.

Federal Communications Commission, Consumer Guide. (2012). *Closed captioning.* Retrieved February 28, 2013, from http://www.fcc.gov/guides/closed-captioning

Fichten, C. S. (1986). Self, other and situation-referent automatic thoughts: Interaction between people who have a physical disability and those who do not. *Cognitive Therapy and Research, 10,* 571–587.

Fine, M., & Asch, A. (Eds.). (1988). *Women with disabilities: Essays in psychology, culture, and politics.* Philadelphia, PA: Temple University Press.

Fine, M., & Asch, A. (2000). Disability beyond stigma: Social interaction, discrimination, and activism. In M. Adams, W. J. Blumenfeld, R. Castaneda, H. W. Hackman, M. L. Peters, & X. Zuniga (Eds.), *Readings for diversity and social justice* (pp. 330–339). New York, NY: Routledge Press.

Fox, J. A., Hatfield, J. P., & Collins, T. C. (2003). Developing the Curriculum, Transformation, and Disability (CTAD) workshop model. In J. L. Higbee (Ed.), *Curriculum transformation and disability: Implementing universal design in higher education* (pp. 23–40). Minneapolis: Center for Research on Developmental Education and Urban Literacy, General College, University of Minnesota.

Franke, A. H., Bérubé, M. F., O'Neil, R. M., & Kurland, J. E. (2012, July 1). Accommodating faculty members who have disabilities. *Academe, 98*(4), 1–13.

Freire, P. (2004). *Pedagogy of the oppressed.* New York, NY: Continuum Publishing.

Gallardo, M. E., & Gibson, J. (2005). *Understanding the therapeutic needs of culturally diverse people with disabilities.* Framingham, MA: Microtraining and Multicultural Development. Retrieved October 11, 2013, from https://www.academicvideostore.com/video/culturally-diverse-individuals-disabilities-therapeutic-needs

General College, University of Minnesota. (Producer). (2002). *Uncertain welcome: Student perspectives on disability and postsecondary education* [Video]. Retrieved October 11, 2013, from http://www.cehd.umn.edu/passit/

Getzel, E. E., & Briel, L. (2006). Pursuing postsecondary educational opportunities for individuals with disabilities. In P. Wehman (Ed.), *Life beyond the classroom: Transition strategies for young people with disabilities* (pp. 355–368). Baltimore, MD: Paul H. Brookes.

Getzel, E. E., & McManus, S. (2005). Expanding support services on campus. In E. E. Getzel & P. Wehman (Eds.), *Going to college: Expanding opportunities for people with disabilities* (pp. 139–154). Baltimore, MD: Paul H. Brookes.

Getzel, E. E., & Thoma, C. (2008). Experiences of college students with disabilities and the importance of self-determination in higher education settings. *Career Development for Exceptional Individuals, 31*(2), 77–84.

Getzel, E. E., & Wehman, P. (Eds.). (2005). *Going to college: Expanding opportunities for people with disabilities.* Baltimore, MD: Paul H. Brookes.

Gibson, J. (2006). Disability and clinical competency: An introduction. *The California Psychologist, 39,* 6–10.

Gibson, J. (2011). Advancing care to clients with disabilities through clinical competency. *The California Psychologist, 44*(4), 23–26.

Gilson, S. F. (2000). Discussion of disability and use of self in the classroom. *Journal of Teaching in Social Work, 20,* 125–136.

Giroux, H. A. (2005). *Border crossings: Cultural workers and the politics of education.* New York, NY: Routledge Press.

Goff, E., & Higbee, J. L. (Eds.). (2008a). *Pedagogy and student services for institutional transformation: Implementation guidebook for student development programs and services.* Minneapolis: Regents of the University of Minnesota by its College of Education and Human Development, University of Minnesota.

Goff, E., & Higbee, J. L. (Eds.). (2008b). *Pedagogy and student services for institutional transformation: Implementation guidebook for faculty and instructional staff.* Minneapolis: Regents of the University of Minnesota by its College of Education and Human Development, University of Minnesota.

Goff, E., & Higbee, J. L. (2008c). Introduction. In J. L. Higbee & E. Goff (Eds.), *Pedagogy and student services for institutional transformation: Implementing universal design in higher education* (pp. 1–8). Minneapolis: Center for Research on Developmental Education and Urban Literacy, University of Minnesota.

Goodman, D. J. (2001). *Promoting diversity and social justice: Educating people from privileged groups.* Thousand Oaks, CA: Sage.

Gordon, B. O., & Rosenblum, K. E. (2001). Bringing disability into the sociological frame: A comparison of disability with race, sex, and sexual orientation statuses. *Disability & Society, 16*(1), 5–19.

Gregg, N. (2009). *Adolescents and adults with learning disabilities and ADHD: Assessment and accommodation.* New York, NY: Guilford.

Griffin, P., & McClintock, M. (1997). History of ableism in Europe and the United States—A selected timeline. In M. Adams, L. A. Bell, & P. Griffin (Eds.), *Teaching for diversity and social justice* (pp. 219–225). New York, NY: Routledge Press.

Grossman, P. D. (2009). Forward with a challenge: Leading our campuses away from the perfect storm. *Journal of Postsecondary Education and Disability, 22*(1), 4–9.

Guckenberger v. Boston University, 957 F. Supp. 306, D. Mass. (1997).

Guckenberger v. Boston University, 974 F. Supp. 106, D. Mass. (1997).

Guckenberger v. Boston University, 8 F. Supp. 2d 82, D. Mass. (1998).

Guillermo, M. S. (2003). *Higher education administrators and students with disabilities: A survey of administrator knowledge and training needs* (Doctoral dissertation). University of San Diego, CA.

Hahn, H. (1988). The politics of physical differences: Disability and discrimination. *Journal of Social Issues, 44*(1), 39–47.

Hahn, H. (1991). Alternative views of empowerment: Social services and civil rights. *Journal of Rehabilitation, 57*(4), 17–19.

Hardiman, R., & Jackson, B. W. (1997). Conceptual foundations for social justice courses. In M. Adams, L. A. Bell, & P. Griffin (Eds.), *Teaching for diversity and social justice: A sourcebook* (pp. 35–66). New York, NY: Routledge Press.

Harper, S. (Ed.). (2008). *Creating inclusive campus environments: For cross-cultural learning and student engagement.* Washington, DC: National Association of Student Personnel Administrators.

Haverkos, P. J. (2011). Finding the union of success and access: A focus on learning for students with disabilities. In P. M. Magolda & M. B. B. Magolda (Eds.), *Contested issues in student affairs: Diverse perspective and respectful dialogue* (pp. 309–315). Sterling, VA: Stylus.

Henderson, C. (2001). *College freshman with disabilities, 2001: A biennial statistical profile.* Washington, DC: American Council of Education, HEATH Resource Center.

Heyward, S. M. (1993). Students' rights and responsibilities. In S. Kroeger & J. Schuck (Eds.), *New Directions for Student Services: No. 64. Responding to disability issues in student affairs* (pp. 17–29). San Francisco, CA: Jossey-Bass.

Higbee, J. L. (Ed.). (2003). *Curriculum transformation and disability: Implementing universal design in higher education.* Minneapolis: Center for Research on Developmental Education and Urban Literacy, General College, University of Minnesota.

Higbee, J. L. (2008). Universal design principles for student development programs and services. In J. L. Higbee & E. Goff (Eds.), *Pedagogy and student services for institutional transformation: Implementing universal design in higher education* (pp. 195–203). Minneapolis: The Regents of the University of Minnesota, Center for Research on Developmental Education and Urban Literacy, College of Education and Human Development, University of Minnesota.

Higbee, J. L. (2012). Creating a culture of inclusion: Respectful, intentional, reflection teaching. Expanding the frame—Applying universal design in higher education, Part III. *ACPA Developments 10*(3). Retrieved February 28, 2013, from http://www2.myacpa.org/developments/fall-2012

Higbee, J. L., & Barajas, H. L. (2007). Building effective places for multicultural learning. *About Campus, 12*(3), 16–22.

Higbee, J. L., & Goff, E. (Eds.). (2008). *Pedagogy and student services for institutional transformation: Implementing universal design in higher education.* Minneapolis: The Regents of the University of Minnesota, Center for Research on Developmental Education and Urban Literacy, College of Education and Human Development, University of Minnesota.

Higbee, J. L., Goff, E., & Schultz, J. L. (2012). Promoting retention through the implementation of integrated multicultural instructional design. *Journal of College Student Retention: Research, Theory and Practice, 14*(3), 291–310.

Higbee, J. L., & Mitchell, A. A. (Eds.). (2009). *Making good on the promise: Student affairs professionals with disabilities.* Lanham, MD: American College Personnel Association and University Press of America.

Higbee, J. L., Schultz, J. L., & Goff, E. (2010). The pedagogy of inclusion: Integrated multicultural instructional design. *Journal of College Reading and Learning, 41*(1), 49–66.

Higher Education Research Institute (HERI). (2012). *CIRP.* Retrieved February 28, 2013, from http://www.heri.ucla.edu/index.php

hooks, b. (1994). *Teaching to transgress: Educating as the practice of freedom.* New York, NY: Routledge Press.

Hughes, B. (2002). Disability and the body. In C. Barnes, M. Oliver, and L. Barton (Eds.), *Disability Studies Today* (pp. 58–76). Cambridge, England: Polity.

Hurley, B. (1991). Accommodating learning disabled students in higher education: Schools' legal obligations under Section 504 of the Rehabilitation Act. *Boston College Law Review, 32*(5), 1051–1103.

Jacoby, B. (1993). Service delivery for a changing student constituency. In M. J. Barr & Associates (Eds.), *The handbook of student affairs administration* (pp. 468–480). San Francisco, CA: Jossey-Bass.

Jarrow, J. (1993). Beyond ramps: New ways of viewing access. In S. Kroeger & J. Schuck (Eds.), *New Directions for Student Services: No. 64. Responding to disability issues in student affairs* (pp. 5–16). San Francisco, CA: Jossey-Bass.

Jenkins v. National Board of Medical Examiners. No. 08–5371 (6th Cir. February 11, 2009). Retrieved October 11, 2013, from http://scholar.google.com/scholar_case? case=10645567018805576106&q=jenkins+v.+national+board+of+medical+examiners& hl=en&as_sdt=2,26&as_vis=1

Johnson, A. G. (2006). *Privilege, power, and difference*. Boston, MA: McGraw-Hill.

Johnson, D. M., & Fox, J. A. (2003). Creating curb cuts in the classroom: Adapting universal design principles to education. In J. L. Higbee (Ed.), *Curriculum transformation and disability: Implementing universal design in higher education* (pp. 7–21). Minneapolis: Center for Research on Developmental Education and Urban Literacy, General College, University of Minnesota.

Jones, S. R. (1996). Toward inclusive theory: Disability as social construction. *NASPA Journal, 33*(4), 347–354.

Jones, S. R., & McEwen, M. K. (2000). A conceptual model of multiple dimensions of identity. *Journal of College Student Development, 41*, 405–414.

Kalivoda, K. (2009). Disability realities: Community, culture, and connection on college campuses. In A. Mitchell & J. Higbee (Eds.), *Making good on the promise: Student affairs professionals with disabilities* (pp. 3–25). Lanham, MD: University Press of America.

Kaplin, W. A., & Lee, B. A. (2007). *The law of higher education* (4th ed.). San Francisco, CA: Jossey-Bass.

Kentucky's Office for the Americans with Disabilities Act (KYADA). (2007). *ADA general information: What does the ADA cover?* Retrieved February 15, 2013, from http://ada.ky.gov/titles.htm

Lerner, D., Amick, B. C., Lee, J. C., Rooney, T., Rogers, W. H., Chang, H., & Berndt, E. R. (2003). Relationship of employee-reported work limitations to work productivity. *Medical Care, 41*(5), 649–659.

Leyser, Y. (1989). A survey of faculty attitudes and accommodations for students with disabilities. *Journal of Postsecondary Education and Disability, 7*(3–4), 97–108.

Leyser, Y., Vogel, S., Wyland, S., & Brulle, A. (1998). Faculty attitudes and practices regarding students with disabilities: Two decades after implementation of Section 504. *Journal on Postsecondary Education and Disability, 13*(3), 5–19.

Liebert, D. T. (2003). The mentally ill and access to higher education: A review of trends, implications, and future possibilities for the Americans with disabilities act and the rehabilitation act. *International Journal of Psychosocial Rehabilitation, 7*. Retrieved October 11, 2011, from http://www.psychosocial.com/IJPR_7/Liebert.html

Lindburg, J. J. (2012). Creating a culture of inclusive leadership: The intersection of student affairs and universal design. Expanding the frame—Applying universal design in higher education, Part III. *ACPA Developments 10*(3). Retrieved October 11, 2013, from http://www2.myacpa.org/developments/fall-2012

Linton, S. (1998). *Claiming disability*. New York: New York University Press.

Linton, S. (2007). *My body politic, a memoir*. Ann Arbor: The University of Michigan Press.

Lombana, J. H. (1989). Counseling persons with disabilities: Summary and projections. *Journal of Counseling and Development, 68*(1), 177–179.

Longmore, P. (2003). *Why I burned my book*. Philadelphia, PA: Temple University Press.

Lyons, M., & Hayes, R. (1993). Student perceptions of persons with psychiatric and other disorders. *The American Journal of Occupational Therapy, 47*, 541–548.

Mackelprang, R. W., & Salsgiver, R. O. (1999). *Disability: A diversity model approach in human service practice*. New York, NY: Brooks/Cole.

Madaus, J. W., Miller, W. K., & Vance, M. L. (2009). Veterans with disabilities in postsecondary education. *Journal of Postsecondary Education and Disability, 22*(1), 10–17.

Marklein, M. B. (2011, October 18). Learning-disabled students get firmer grip on college. *USA Today*. Retrieved February 12, 2013, from http://usatoday30.usatoday .com/news/education/story/2011--10--17/college-andlearning-disabilities/50807620/1

Marks, D. (1999). *Disability: Controversial debates and psychosocial perspectives*. New York, NY: Routledge Press.

Massie-Burrell, T. (2009). An intersection of multiple identities: Congenital limb amputation. In J. Higbee & A. Mitchell (Eds.), *Making good on the promise: Student affairs professionals with disabilities* (pp. 58–61). Washington, DC: American College Personnel Association and University Press of America.

McCarthy, D. (2007). Teaching self-advocacy to students with disabilities. *About Campus, 12*(5), 10–16.

McCarthy, D. (2011). What are the implications of providing special considerations to particular students? In P. M. Magolda & M. B. B. Magolda (Eds.), *Contested issues in student affairs: Diverse perspective and respectful dialogue* (pp. 298–308). Sterling, VA: Stylus.

McDonald-Dennis, C. (2009). An unexpected additional identity: Human Immunodeficiency Virus (HIV). In J. Higbee & A. Mitchell (Eds.), *Making good on the promise: Student affairs professionals with disabilities* (pp. 62–69).Washington, DC: American College Personnel Association and University Press of America.

McGuire, J. M., Scot, S. S., & Shaw, S. F. (2006, May/June). Universal design and its applications in educational environments. *Remedial and Special Education, 27*(3), 166–175.

McRuer, R. (2006). *Cultural signs of queerness and disability*. New York: New York University Press.

Meyer, A., Myers, K., Walmsley, A., & Laux, S. (2012). Academic accommodations: Perceptions, knowledge and awareness among college students without disabilities. *Education, 2*(5), 174–182.

Michalko, R. (2002). *The difference that disability makes*. Philadelphia, PA: Temple University Press.

Michigan State University (MSU). (2013). *Southeastern Community College v. Davis*. Retrieved February 15, 2013, from http://www.animallaw.info/cases/causfd99sct2361.htm

Miles, D. (2010). *Officials tout post-9/11 bill benefits*. Retrieved October 11, 2013, from http://www.defense.gov/news/newsarticle.aspx?id=61337

Mullins, A. (2009). *It's not fair having 12 pairs of legs*. TED Talks. Retrieved November 1, 2012, from http://www.ted.com/talks/aimee_mullins_prosthetic_aesthetics.html

Murdick, N. L., Gartin, B. C., & Crabtree, T. (2007). *Special education law* (2nd ed.). Upper Saddle River, NJ: Pearson.

Myers, K. (2008a). Incorporating UID in higher education administration courses: A case study. In S. Burgstahler & R. Cory (Eds.), *Universal design in postsecondary education, from principles to practice* (pp. 157–164). Cambridge, MA: Harvard Education Press.

Myers, K. (2008b). Using learning reconsidered to reinvent disability education. *About Campus, 13*(2), 2–9.

Myers, K. (2009a). A new vision for disability education: Moving on from the add-on. *About Campus, 14*(5), 15–21.

Myers, K. (2009b). *College students with visual disabilities: Preferences for effective interaction.* Saarbrücken, Germany: VDM Verlag Publications.

Myers, K. (2012). Creating a culture of inclusion: Listening to the voices of people with disabilities. Expanding the frame—Applying universal design in higher education, Part II. *ACPA Developments, 10*(2). Retrieved October 11, 2013, from http://www2.myacpa.org/developments/summer-2012

Myers, K., & Bastian, J. (2010). Understanding communication preferences of college students with visual disabilities. *Journal of College Student Development, 51*(3), 265–278.

Myers, K., Jenkins, J., & Pousson, M. (2009). Social norms and disability. *ACPA Developments.* Retrieved February 28, 2013, from http://www.myacpa.org/pub/developments/archives/2009/Summer/article.php?content=myersa

Myers, K., Spudich, C., Spudich, D., & Laux, S. (2012). Saving face: Inclusive communication with college students with disabilities using politeness and face negotiation. *Journal of Diversity Management, 7*(2), 97–108.

National Federation for the Blind. (2013). *Braille initiative.* Retrieved from https://nfb.org/braille-initiative

National Institute of Mental Health (NIMH). (2013). *The number count: Mental disorders in America.* Retrieved February 27, 2013, from http://www.nimh.nih.gov/health/publications/the-numbers-count-mental-disorders-in-america/index.shtml

North Carolina State University. (2008). *The principles of universal design.* Retrieved October 8, 2013, from http://www.ncsu.edu/ncsu/design/cud/about_ud/about_ud.htm

Office for Civil Rights. (1998a). *Auxiliary aids and services for postsecondary students with disabilities.* Retrieved February 28, 2013, from http://www2.ed.gov/about/offices/list/ocr/docs/auxaids.html

Office for Civil Rights. (1998b). *Title IX and sex discrimination.* Retrieved October 11, 2013, from http://www2.ed.gov/about/offices/list/ocr/docs/tix_dis.html

Oliver, M. (1996). *Understanding disability, from theory to practice.* London, United Kingdom: Macmillan.

Olkin, R. (2003). Women with disabilities. In J. C. Chrisler, C. Golden, & P. D. Rozee (Eds.), *Lectures on the psychology of women* (3rd ed., pp. 144–157). New York, NY: McGraw-Hill.

Olney, M. F., & Brockelman, K. F. (2003). Out of the disability closet: Strategic use of perception management by select university students with disabilities. *Disability & Society, 18,* 35–50.

Palombi, B. (2000). Recruitment and admission of students with disabilities. In H. A. Belch (Ed.), *New Directions for Student Services No. 91. Serving students with disabilities* (pp. 31–39). San Francisco, CA: Jossey-Bass.

Pederson, P. (1988). *Handbook for developing multicultural awareness.* Alexandria, VA: American Association for Counseling and Development.

Phinney, J. S. (1989). Stages of ethnic identity development in minority group adolescents. *Journal of Early Adolescence, 9,* 34–49.

Pliner, S., & Johnson, J. (2004). Historical, theoretical, and foundational principles of universal instructional design in higher education. *Equity and Excellence in Education, 37,* 105–113.

Pushkin v. Regents of the University of Colorado, 658 F.2d 1372 (10th Cir. 1981).

RAND Center for Military Health Policy Research. (2008). *Invisible wounds: Mental health and cognitive care needs of America's returning veterans.* Retrieved February 21, 2013, from http://www.rand.org/pubs/research_briefs/RB9336

Raue, K., & Lewis, L. (2011). *Students with disabilities at degree-granting postsecondary institutions* (NCES 2011–018). United States Department of Education, National Center for Education Statistics. Washington, DC: Government Printing Office.

Rauscher, L., & McClintock, M. (1997). Ableism curriculum design. In M. Adams, L. A. Bell, & P. Griffin (Eds.), *Teaching for diversity and social justice* (pp. 198–229). New York, NY: Routledge Press.

Rehabilitation Act of 1973, Sec 504 (1973). Retrieved October 11, 2013, from http://www2.ed.gov/policy/speced/reg/narrative.html

Reilly, V. J., & Davis, T. (2005). Understanding the regulatory environment. In E. E. Getzel & P. Wehman (Eds.), *Going to college: Expanding opportunities for people with disabilities* (pp. 25–48). Baltimore, MD: Paul H. Brookes.

Rose, B. (2013). *Nine cases that have shaped disability services in higher education.* Retrieved February 14, 2013, from http://gwired.gwu.edu/dss/faculty/legal/ninecases/

Rudolph, F. (1990). *The American college and university: A history.* Athens: The University of Georgia Press.

Sachs, D., & Schreuer, N. (2011). Inclusion of students with disabilities in higher education: Performance and participation in student's experiences. *Disability Studies Quarterly, 31*(2). Retrieved February 11, 2013, from http://dsq-sds.org/article/view/1593/1561

Sandler, B. R. (1997). *Too strong for a woman—The five words that created title IX.* Retrieved February 16, 2013, from http://www.bernicesandler.com/id44.htm

Sandler, M. (2008). *College confluence with ADD.* Naperville, IL: Sourcebooks.

Scheer, J. (1994). Culture and disability: An anthropological point of view. In E. J. Trickett, R. J. Watts, D. Birman (Eds.), *Human diversity: Perspectives on people in context* (pp. 244–260). San Francisco, CA: Jossey-Bass.

Schlossberg, N. K. (1989). Marginality and mattering: Key issues in building community. In D. C. Roberts (Ed.), *New Directions for Student Services: No. 48. Designing campus activities to foster a sense of community* (pp. 5–15). San Francisco, CA: Jossey-Bass.

Schlossberg, N. K., Waters, E. B., & Goodman, J. (1995). *Counseling adults in transition* (2nd ed.). New York, NY: Springer.

Shackelford, A. L. (2009). Documenting the needs of student veterans with disabilities: Intersection roadblocks, solutions, and legal realities. *Journal of Postsecondary Education and Disability, 22*(1), 36–42.

Silver, P., Bourke, A., & Strehorn, K. C. (1998). Universal instructional design in higher education: An approach for inclusion. *Equity and Excellence in Education, 31*(2), 47–51.

Snyder, T., & Dillow, S. (2010). *Digest of Education Statistics 2009* (NCES 2010–013; Table 231). Washington, DC: National Center for Education Statistics, Institute of Education Sciences, United States Department of Education.

Society for Disability Studies (SDS). (2013). *SDS Mission.* Retrieved October 11, 2013, from http://www.disstudies.org/about/mission-and-history

Solorzano, D., Ceja, M., & Yosso, T. (2000). Critical race theory, racial microaggressions, and campus racial climate: The experiences of African American college students. *Journal of Negro Education, 69,* 60–73.

Southeastern Community College v. Davis, 442 U.S. 397 (1979).

Strange, C. C., & Banning, J. H. (2001). *Educating by design: Creating campus learning environments that work.* San Francisco, CA: Jossey-Bass.

Sue, D. W., & Capodilupo, C. M. (2008). Racial, gender and sexual orientation microaggressions: Implications for counseling and psychotherapy. In D. W. Sue & D. Sue (Eds.), *Counseling the culturally diverse: Theory and practice* (5th ed., pp. 298–314). Hoboken, NJ: John Wiley & Sons.

Sue, D. W., & Sue, D. (2008). *Counseling the culturally diverse.* Hoboken, NJ: John Wiley & Sons.

Texas A&M. (2013). *Americans with Disabilities Act.* Retrieved February 14, 2013, from http://bushlibrary.tamu.edu/features/2010-ada/

Thompson, M. (2012). Creating a culture of inclusion: Shifting the disability frame, Part III. *ACPA Developments, 10*(1). Retrieved February 28, 2013, from http://www2.myacpa.org/developments/spring-2012

Titleix.info. (2013). *History of Title IX.* Retrieved February 26, 2013, from http://www.titleix.info/History/History-Overview.aspx

Tregoning, M. (2009). Being an ally in language use. In J. Higbee & A. Mitchell (Eds.), *Making good on the promise: Student affairs professionals with disabilities* (pp. 171–176). Washington, DC: American College Personnel Association and University Press of America.

Trickett, E. J., Watts, R. J., & Birman, D. (1994). Toward an overarching framework for diversity. In E. J. Tricket, R. J. Watts, & D. Birman (Eds.), *Human diversity: Perspectives of people in context* (pp. 7–26). San Francisco, CA: Jossey-Bass.

Tripoli, L., Mellard, D. F., & Kurth, N. K. (2004). *The individual accommodations model (IAM): Accommodating students with disabilities in postsecondary settings.* Lawrence: Center for Research on Learning, University of Kansas.

Troiano, P. F. (2003). College students and learning disability: Elements of self-style. *Journal of College Student Development, 44*(3), 404–419.

21st Century Communications and Video Accessibility Act of 2010, Pub. L. No. 111–260 (2010). Retrieved October 11, 2013, from http://www.gpo.gov/fdsys/pkg/PLAW-111publ260/html/PLAW-111publ260.htm

Unger, D. D. (2002). Employer's attitudes toward people with disabilities in the workforce: Myths or realities? *Focus on Autism and other Developmental Disabilities, 17,* 2–10.

United Nations (UN). (2006). *Convention on the Rights of Persons With Disabilities.* New York, NY: Author. Retrieved October 11, 2013, from http://www.un.org/disabilities/convention/conventionfull.shtml

United States Department of Education, National Center for Education Statistics (ED NCES). (2006). *Profile of Undergraduates in U.S. Postsecondary Education Institutions: 2003–2004 With a Special Analysis of Community College Students* (NCES 2006184), Section 6. Retrieved October 22, 2013, from http://nces.ed.gov/pubsearch/pubsinfo.asp?pubid=2006184

United States Department of Education, National Center for Education Statistics (ED NCES). (2012a). *Digest of Education Statistics, 2011* (2012–001), Chapter 3. Retrieved from http://nces.ed.gov/pubs2012/2012001.pdf

United States Department of Education, National Center for Education Statistics (ED NCES). (2012b). *Digest of Education Statistics, 2011* (NCES 2012–001), Table 242. Retrieved from http://nces.ed.gov/pubs2012/2012001.pdf

United States Department of Health and Human Services. (2006). *Your Rights under Section 504 of the Rehabilitation Act.* Retrieved February 15, 2013, from http://www.hhs.gov/ocr/civilrights/resources/factsheets/504.pdf

United States Department of Justice. (2002). *Americans with Disabilities Act: Questions and Answers.* Retrieved February 15, 2013, from http://www.ada.gov/q&aeng02.htm

United States Equal Employment Opportunity Commission (EEOC). (1997). *The ADA: Questions and Answers.* Retrieved February 16, 2013, from http://www.eeoc.gov/facts/adaqa1.html

United States Senate Committee on the Judiciary. (2013). *The Civil Rights Act of 1964.* Retrieved February 14, 2013, from http://www.judiciary.senate.gov/about/history/CivilRightsAct.cfm

University of Alabama v. Garrett, 531 U.S. 356 (2001).

University of Massachusetts Amherst. (2011). *Accommodations and services for students.* Retrieved February 27, 2013, from http://www.umass.edu/disability/students.html

Upton, T. D., Harper, D. C., & Wadsworth, J. (2005). Postsecondary attitudes toward persons with disabilities: A comparison of college students with and without disabilities. *Journal of Applied Rehabilitation Counseling, 36,* 24–31.

Washington, J., & Evans, N. J. (1991). Becoming an ally. In N. J. Evans & V. A. Wall (Eds.), *Beyond tolerance: Gays, lesbians, and bisexuals on campus* (pp. 195–204). Washington, DC: American College Personnel Association.

Wells, S. J. (2001). Is the ADA working? *HR Magazine, 45*(4), 38–46.

White House Press Secretary. (1990). *Fact Sheet: The Americans with Disabilities of 1990.* Retrieved February 15, 2013, from http://bushlibrary.tamu.edu/features/2010-ada/FactSheet_1.pdf

Wieland, A. (2009). An invisible identity: Learning disability. In J. Higbee & A. Mitchell (Eds.), *Making good on the promise: Student affairs professionals with disabilities* (pp. 70–76). Washington, DC: American College Personnel Association and University Press of America.

Wijeyesinghe, C. L., Griffin, P., & Love, B. (1997). Racism curriculum design. In M. Adams, L. A. Bell, & P. Griffin (Eds.), *Teaching for diversity and social justice: A sourcebook* (pp. 82–109). New York, NY: Routledge Press.

Wilson, J. (1988). Understanding the Vietnam veteran. In F. Ochberg (Ed.), *Post-traumatic therapy and victims of violence* (pp. 227–254). New York, NY: Brunne/Mazel.

World Wide Web Consortium (W3C). (2012). *Standards.* Retrieved February 27, 2013, from http://www.w3.org/standards/

Wynne v. Tufts University School of Medicine, 976 F.2d 791 (1992).

Yost, D. (2008, March 27). Discrimination takes on all forms. *Independent: Southwestern Minnesota's Daily Newspaper.* Retrieved February 15, 2013, from http://www.marshallindependent.com/page/content.detail/id/500479.html?nav=5015

Yuker, H. E. (1994). Variables that influence attitudes toward people with disabilities: Conclusions from the data. In D. S. Dunn (Ed.), *Psychosocial perspectives on disability* [Special issue]. *Journal of Social Behavior and Personality, 9,* 3–22.

Name Index

Fichten, C. S., 39
Fine, M., 51–53
Fox, J. A., 95
Franke, A. H., 43
Freire, P., 80

G

Gallardo, M. E., 32
Gamson, Z. F., 95
Gartin, B. C., 87
Getzel, E. E., 33, 39, 41, 43, 84
Gibson, J., 5, 32, 56, 75, 86, 89
Gilson, S. F., 6
Giroux, H. A., 81, 82
Goff, E., 5, 94, 96, 102
Goodman, D. J., 71, 73
Goodman, J., 58
Gordon, B. O., 61
Gregg, N., 37, 38, 48
Griffin, P., 50, 51, 70
Grossman, P. D., 37
Guillermo, M. S., 44

H

Hahn, H., 52
Hardiman, R., 82
Harper, D. C., 4, 39
Harper, S., 61
Hatfield, J. P., 95
Haverkos, P. J., 64
Hayes, R., 39
Henderson, C., 37
Herriott, T., 34, 54, 64, 72
Heyward, S. M., 17, 19
Higbee, J. L., 5, 9, 43, 51, 52, 72, 88, 89, 95–98, 102, 108
hooks, b., 69, 81
Hurley, B., 21, 22, 25

J

Jackson, B. W., 82
Jacoby, B., 54
Jarrow, J., 15–17, 37
Jenkins, J., 4, 42
Johnson, A. G., 83

Johnson, D. M., 95
Johnson, J., 3
Jones, S. R., 2, 51–53, 55, 61, 73, 83

K

Kalivoda, K., 59
Kaplin, W. A., 21–28
Kurland, J. E., 43
Kurth, N. K., 4
Laux, S., 4, 39, 89

L

Lee, B. A., 21–28
Lee, J. C., 40
Lerner, D., 40
Lewis, L., 5, 37, 38, 45
Leyser, Y., 43, 44
Liebert, D. T., 24
Lindburg, J. J., 97, 98
Linton, S., 2, 3, 33, 50, 54, 86, 88, 89
Lombana, J. H., 86
Longmore, P., 52, 53, 98
Love, B., 70
Lyons, M., 39

M

Mackelprang, R. W., 51
Madaus, J. W., 65, 66
Marklein, M. B., 41, 43
Marks, D., 46
Massie-Burrell, T., 33
McCarthy, D., 41, 60, 62, 63, 83
McClintock, M., 50, 51, 83
McDonald-Dennis, C., 33
McEwen, M. K., 73
McGuire, J. M., 35, 43, 94
McManus, S., 33, 39
McRuer, R., 104
Mellard, D. F., 4
Meyer, A., 4, 39
Michalko, R., 51, 52
Miles, D., 37
Miller, W. K., 65, 66
Mitchell, A. A., 9, 43, 51, 52, 72, 89, 97
Mullins, A., 3, 10, 106

Murdick, N. L., 87
Myers, K. A., 4, 11, 34, 39–44, 54, 55, 64, 88, 89, 98, 102, 107, 108

O
Oliver, M., 6
Olkin, R., 55
Olney, M. F., 4
O'Neil, R. M., 43

P
Palombi, B., 34
Pederson, P., 34
Peters, M. L., 53, 54, 60
Phinney, J. S., 75
Pliner, S., 3
Pousson, M., 4, 42

R
Raue, K., 5, 37, 38, 45
Rauscher, L., 83
Reilly, V. J., 43
Rogers, W. H., 40
Rooney, T., 40
Rose, B., 23, 25–27
Rosenblum, K. E., 61
Rudolph, F., 64

S
Sachs, D., 40
Sagendorf, K., 46, 86, 87
Salsgiver, R. O., 51
Sandler, B. R., 16
Sandler, M., 38
Scheer, J., 52
Schlossberg, N. K., 5, 53, 58, 59, 64
Schoen, S., 108
Schreuer, N., 40
Schultz, J. L., 96
Scot, S. S., 94
Segoria, J., 66
Shackelford, A. L., 65, 66
Shaw, S. F., 35, 43, 95

Silver, P., 95
Snyder, T., 2, 38
Solorzano, D., 62
Souma, A., 9, 46, 70
Spudich, C., 89
Spudich, D., 89
Strange, C. C., 41, 103
Strehorn, K. C., 95
Sue, D., 32
Sue, D. W., 32, 62
Thoma, C., 39, 41, 43

T
Thompson, M., 98
Tregoning, M., 3, 33, 87, 89, 98
Trickett, E. J., 53
Tripoli, L., 4
Troiano, P. F., 55

U
Unger, D. D., 45
Upton, T. D., 4, 39

V
Vance, M. L., 65, 66
Vogel, S., 43

W
Wadsworth, J., 4, 39
Walmsley, A., 4, 39
Washington, J., 80
Waters, E. B., 58
Watts, R. J., 53
Wehman, P., 84
Wells, S. J., 45
Wieland, A., 33
Wijeyesinghe, C. L., 70
Wilson, J., 38
Wyland, S., 43

Y
Yosso, T., 62
Yost, D., 13
Yuker, H. E., 39

Subject Index

B

Behaviors/attitudes, for people with disabilities, 2–3, 4, 59–63; language and, 3

Bishop's six-step model, 79–80

BLR. *See* Business and Legal Resources (BLR)

Boston University, Guckenberger v., 26–27

Broido Model of Social Justice Ally Development, 75–77

Business and Legal Resources (BLR), 21

C

California State University Northridge (CSUN), 46, 47; International Technology and Persons with Disabilities Conference, 46

Call to action; global, 107–108; personal, 106–107

CAS. *See* Council on the Advancement of Standards (CAS)

Celebrities, with disabilities, 106

Center for Universal Design, 93–94

CIRP. *See* Cooperative Institutional Research Program (CIRP)

Civil Rights Act of 1964, 2, 15; Title IX of, 15, 16

Claiming Disability (Linton), 88–89

Cognitively disabled persons; interacting with, tips for, 92–93

College campuses, disability of, 31–48; ADA and, 35; *See also* Higher education, disability in

Communication, strategies and tips, 89–93

Convention on the Rights of Persons With Disabilities, 108

Cooperative Institutional Research Program (CIRP), 37

Cornell University, 46; Employment and Disability Institute, 46; World Wide Web Consortium (W3C), 46

Council on the Advancement of Standards (CAS), 35, 63

CSUN. *See* California State University Northridge (CSUN)

Curriculum, disability education in, 103, 104

CVAA. *See* 21st Century Communications and Accessibility Act (CVAA)

D

DAC. *See* Disability Access Consultants (DAC)

Davis, Southeastern Community College v., 22

DEAF Inc., 89

Deaf persons; interacting with, tips for, 91–92

Development theories, allies, 75; Bishop's six-step model, 79–80; Broido Model of Social Justice Ally Development, 75–77; Edward's Model for Aspiring Social Justice Ally Identity Development, 77–79; Washington and Evans' Model, 80

Development theories, students with disabilities, 55–56; Disability Identity Development Model, 56–58; on learning disabilities, 55; Theory of Marginality and Mattering, 59; Transition Theory, 58–59

Disabilities, Opportunities, Internetworking, and Technology (DO IT) program, 46; website, 46

Disability; defined, 6–8, 14; and diversity, 32; early policies, 15–16; in higher education, 32–35; and identity development, 32; invisible or "hidden," 4; learning, 37; models of, 50–55; onset of, 57–58; psychological, 37–38; social norming for, 42; visible, 14; "in-group" and "out-of-group" circumstances related to, 33; *See also* Allies; Behaviors/attitudes, for people with disabilities; Language, disability

Disability Access Consultants (DAC), 18

Disability education, 2, 3, 4; in curriculum, 103, 104; new vision for, 101–104

Disability Identity Development Model; stages of, 56–58

University of Washington, 46; DO IT
  program, 46–47

V

Veterans with disabilities, 65–66
Visible disability, 14
Visually impaired person, 91; interacting
  with, tips for, 91

W

W3C. *See* World Wide Web Consortium
  (W3C)
Washington and Evans's model, 80
World Wide Web Consortium (W3C),
  46–47
*Wynne v. Tufts University School of
  Medicine*, 25–26

About the Authors

Karen A. Myers, PhD, is an associate professor and director of the higher education administration graduate program at Saint Louis University and the director of the award-winning international disability education project, *Allies for Inclusion: The Ability Exhibit.* She has been a college teacher and an administrator since 1979, is a national disability consultant and trainer, and teaches her self-designed graduate course, Disability in Higher Education and Society. She is the recipient of the ACPA College Student Educators International Voice of Inclusion Medallion, Annuit Coeptis Senior Professional Award, ACPA Foundation Diamond Honoree, and cofounder of the ACPA Standing Committee on Disability.

Jaci Jenkins Lindburg, PhD, is the assistant director of academic affairs for the Division of Continuing Studies and a member of the faculty in women's and gender studies at the University of Nebraska-Omaha. Previously, she has led student development and leadership programs at McKendree University (Illinois) and Washburn University (Kansas). Her additional research interests include college student curiosity and transfer student adjustment. She is involved in the ACPA organization, serving on the Editorial Board of the *Developments* publication, as well as sitting on several Standing Committee Directorates, including the Standing Committee on Disability. She is the recipient of the ACPA Annuit Coeptis Emerging Professional Award, Outstanding New Professional Award, and Disability Ally Award.

Danielle M. Nied, MS, is the assistant director for housing and residence life for leadership and training and PhD student in the higher education program at Saint Louis University. She is also a two-time chair of the Standing Committee for Lesbian, Gay, Bisexual, and Transgender Awareness with ACPA College Student Educators International. Danielle has a strong commitment to residential curriculum, peer education, and multicultural education. Her research interests include identity development, identity performance, and neoliberalism in higher education. Previously, Danielle held positions at the University of Maryland and Colorado State University. She received her master's in College Student Personnel from Western Illinois University.

About the ASHE Higher Education Report Series

Since 1983, the ASHE (formerly ASHE-ERIC) Higher Education Report Series has been providing researchers, scholars, and practitioners with timely and substantive information on the critical issues facing higher education. Each monograph presents a definitive analysis of a higher education problem or issue, based on a thorough synthesis of signifi cant literature and institutional experiences. Topics range from planning to diversity and multiculturalism, to performance indicators, to curricular innovations. The mission of the Series is to link the best of higher education research and practice to inform decision making and policy. The reports connect conventional wisdom with research and are designed to help busy individuals keep up with the higher education literature. Authors are scholars and practitioners in the academic community. Each report includes an executive summary, review of the pertinent literature, descriptions of eff ective educational practices, and a summary of key issues to keep in mind to improve educational policies and practice.

The Series is one of the most peer reviewed in higher education. A National Advisory Board made up of ASHE members reviews proposals. A National Review Board of ASHE scholars and practitioners reviews completed manuscripts. Six monographs are published each year and they are approximately 144 pages in length. The reports are widely disseminated through Jossey-Bass and John Wiley & Sons, and they are available online to subscribing institutions through Wiley Online Library (http://wileyonlinelibrary.com).

Call for Proposals

The ASHE Higher Education Report Series is actively looking for proposals. We encourage you to contact one of the editors, Dr. Kelly Ward (kaward@wsu.edu) or Dr. Lisa Wolf-Wendel (lwolf@ku.edu), with your ideas.

ORDER FORM SUBSCRIPTION AND SINGLE ISSUES

DISCOUNTED BACK ISSUES:

Use this form to receive 20% off all back issues of *ASHE Higher Education Report*.
All single issues priced at **$23.20** (normally $29.00)

TITLE	ISSUE NO.	ISBN
_____	_____	_____
_____	_____	_____
_____	_____	_____

Call 888-378-2537 or see mailing instructions below. When calling, mention the promotional code JBNND to receive your discount. For a complete list of issues, please visit www.josseybass.com/go/aehe

SUBSCRIPTIONS: (1 YEAR, 6 ISSUES)

☐ New Order   ☐ Renewal

U.S.	☐ Individual: $174	☐ Institutional: $327
CANADA/MEXICO	☐ Individual: $174	☐ Institutional: $387
ALL OTHERS	☐ Individual: $210	☐ Institutional: $438

Call 888-378-2537 or see mailing and pricing instructions below.
Online subscriptions are available at www.onlinelibrary.wiley.com

ORDER TOTALS:

Issue / Subscription Amount: $ _____

Shipping Amount: $ _____
(for single issues only – subscription prices include shipping)

Total Amount: $ _____

SHIPPING CHARGES:	
First Item	$6.00
Each Add'l Item	$2.00

(No sales tax for U.S. subscriptions. Canadian residents, add GST for subscription orders. Individual rate subscriptions must be paid by personal check or credit card. Individual rate subscriptions may not be resold as library copies.)

BILLING & SHIPPING INFORMATION:

☐ **PAYMENT ENCLOSED:** *(U.S. check or money order only. All payments must be in U.S. dollars.)*

☐ **CREDIT CARD:**   ☐ VISA   ☐ MC   ☐ AMEX

Card number _____ Exp. Date_____

Card Holder Name_____ Card Issue # _____

Signature _____ Day Phone_____

☐ **BILL ME:** *(U.S. institutional orders only. Purchase order required.)*

Purchase order # _____
Federal Tax ID 13559302 • GST 89102-8052

Name_____

Address_____

Phone_____ E-mail_____

Copy or detach page and send to: **John Wiley & Sons, One Montgomery Street, Suite 1200, San Francisco, CA 94104-4594**

Order Form can also be faxed to: **888-481-2665**

PROMO JBNND